HIGHE
AT THE
OF DISRUPTION

Great Debates in Higher Education is a series of short, accessible books addressing key challenges to and issues in Higher Education, on a national and international level. These books are research informed but debate driven. They are intended to be relevant to a broad spectrum of researchers, students, and administrators in higher education, and are designed to help us unpick and assess the state of higher education systems, policies, and social and economic impacts.

Recently published in this series:

Challenging the Teaching Excellence Framework: Diversity Deficits in Higher Education Evaluations

Amanda French and Kate Carruthers Thomas

Leadership of Historically Black Colleges and Universities: A What Not to Do Guide for HBCU Leaders

Johnny D. Jones

The Fully Functioning University

Tom Bourner, Asher Rospigliosi, and Linda Heath

A Brief History of Credit in UK Higher Education: Laying Siege to the Ivory Tower

Wayne Turnbull

Degendering Leadership in Higher Education

Barret Katuna

Perspectives on Access to Higher Education

Sam Broadhead, Rosemarie Davis, and Anthony Hudson

Cultural Journeys in Higher Education: Student Voices and Narratives

Jan Bamford and Lucy Pollard

Radicalization and Counter-radicalization in Higher Education

Catherine McGlynn and Shaun McDaid

Refugees in Higher Education: Debate, Discourse, and Practice

Jacqueline Stevenson and Sally Baker

The Marketization of English Higher Education: A Policy Analysis of a Risk-Based System

Colin McCaig

Access to Success and Social Mobility through Higher Education: A Curate's Egg?

Edited by Stuart Billingham

Evaluating Scholarship and Research Impact: History, Practices, and Policy Development

Jeffrey W. Alstete, Nicholas J. Beutell, and John P. Meyer

Sexual Violence on Campus: Power-Conscious Approaches to Awareness, Prevention, and Response

Chris Linder

Higher Education, Access, and Funding: The United Kingdom in International Perspective

Edited by Sheila Riddell, Sarah Minty, Elisabet Weedon, and Susan Whittaker

British Universities in the Brexit Moment: Political, Economic, and Cultural Implications

Mike Finn

Challenging the Teaching Excellence Framework: Diversity Deficits in Higher Education Evaluations

Edited by Kate Carruthers Thomas and Amanda French

HIGHER EDUCATION AT THE CROSSROADS OF DISRUPTION

The University of the 21st Century

BY

ANDREAS KAPLAN

Dean ESCP Business School, France

United Kingdom – North America – Japan – India
Malaysia – China

Emerald Publishing Limited
Howard House, Wagon Lane, Bingley BD16 1WA, UK

First edition 2021

Reprints and permissions service
Contact: permissions@emeraldinsight.com

British Library Cataloguing in Publication Data
A catalogue record for this book is available from the British Library

ISBN: 978-1-80071-504-2 (Print)
ISBN: 978-1-80071-501-1 (Online)
ISBN: 978-1-80071-503-5 (Epub)

Printed and bound by CPI Group (UK) Ltd, Croydon, CR0 4YY

ISOQAR certified Management System, awarded to Emerald for adherence to Environmental standard ISO 14001:2004.

INVESTOR IN PEOPLE

CONTENTS

PREFACE

> Nothing is constant except change
>
> –Heraclitus of Ephesus

The ancient Greek philosopher Heraclitus once explained that no man ever can step into the same river twice, as the current constantly flows, constantly changing the river. Or, put differently, "Nothing is constant except change." Universities, though, have long been viewed as resistant to change, monolithic, and highly inflexible.

This unflattering image of higher education has been shaken up with the unprecedented Covid-19 crisis, compelling universities worldwide to move their entire curricula online, in many cases within just days. Higher education impressively pivoted to be adaptable and flexible in an emergency.

The sector's transformation, however, has been ongoing for some time now. Its digitalization, but also general societal, economic, and ecological developments have led to higher education institutions undergoing profound changes. Therefore we can say that higher education is at the crossroads of disruption, thus shaping the university of the twenty-first century.

1

WHY, WHEN, WHAT, WHO, WHERE

While universities are at the forefront of innovation and research in nearly all fields from archeology to biotech, they often appear to fail to do likewise in terms of their very survival. While higher education is resistant to change and extremely risk averse (Kaplan, 2020a), several signs indicate that the sector might be at the crossroads of disruption. Change is in the air, with venture capitalists investing massively in higher education (Straumsheim, 2015) and some of the brightest professors themselves moving into EdTech (educational technology), slowly but surely changing the rules of the game. In light thereof, it actually might be risky *not* to embrace the sector's transformation and potential disruption toward the university of the twenty-first century.

In this introduction, which is framed by the five Ws (Why, When, What, Who, and Where), firstly I'll explain *why* turmoil and transition are occurring in higher education, and I'll address several transformations that universities are currently undergoing. Secondly, I will talk about *when* this book was written, i.e., during the Covid-19 crisis, which is having an enormous impact on higher education, specifically with respect to distance instruction. In the third section, I'll give an overview of *what* you can expect to learn herein, briefly explaining the chapters' contents as well as the case studies at the end of each main chapter. Then I'll give you an idea of *who* I am or my credentials as a researcher as well as rector and dean of a European business school. Finally, the *where* will be addressed, i.e., Europe and elsewhere, with my knowledge mainly based on the "old continent," while insights from elsewhere also enrich this work.

1.1 WHY: TRANSITION AND TURMOIL

For some time now, universities have faced new societal and economic realities necessitating their (profound) transformation, even further underscored and spurred by the Covid-19 crisis, as we will see further on. Multifaceted challenges appear on the horizon, as today's higher education sector is increasingly global, diverse, and crowded (Pucciarelli & Kaplan, 2016).

Most discussions of the current and future state of the university agree on several points. Firstly, business practices are increasingly becoming acceptable in higher education, with some even advocating for adapting pure market logic to higher education (Gibbs & Murphy, 2009). Many universities' economics are no longer working in this new reality. Costs are almost exponentially increasing, which via tuition is transferred to families finding themselves in debt for years and even decades. While this is especially true in the United States, other locales' university tuitions are on the rise. In response, universities are employing competitive strategies to analyze drivers of change, to come up with commensurate responses, and to devise guidelines and policies that enable necessary evolution to take place sooner rather than later.

In general, universities have three basic missions: teaching, research, and public service. While these missions have always been in conflict with one another (Altbach, Reisberg, & Rumbley, 2009), tensions now have increased severalfold. On the one hand, to survive, higher education is compelled to behave like for-profit entities, placing weight on generating revenues and margins. On the other hand, it is still incumbent upon universities to operate as nonprofits, prioritizing their mission of public service (Council of the European Union, 2014).

As higher education institutions are looking for ways to cut costs and increase revenues, they are faced with a multitude of pressures (which in many cases themselves incur additional costs): new technologies and linked infrastructures enabling the delivery of high-quality online courses; a changing society and economy that demand new skills and certification methods; educational start-ups, corporate universities, and EdTech entering the sector; ever-more-demanding accreditation bodies and requirements in order to rank high in all parameters; and finally, governments allotting less and less funding to higher education, to mention just a few. All of these phenomena generate transition and turmoil, shaking up the world of higher education and compelling it to search for new ways to "do business" (Kaplan & Pucciarelli, 2016).

1.2 WHEN: CORONA AND CRISIS

The sector's digitalization has been an issue in higher education for years, if not decades. With the advent of MOOCs (Massive Open Online Courses) and SPOCs (Small Private Online Courses), this issue is again at the forefront. In an article published in *Wired* in 2012, Sebastian Thrun, founder of online course provider Udacity, predicted that many universities would not survive as a result of online courses provided on platforms such as his own (Leckart, 2012). While Thrun's prediction has not materialized, until the spring semester 2020, higher education dragged its feet on entering the virtual sphere on a large scale. University administration, not necessarily familiar with the online world, was also scared off by high investment costs. Neither were professors keen to go online, on pedagogical or other grounds (Kaplan, 2020a).

Then in 2020, corona and a nearly unprecedented health crisis hit, rendering possible what many players in the sector believed impossible: Universities went entirely online almost overnight. Obviously, not everything went smoothly, and many were rather "quick and dirty" solutions that students would likely have ordinarily criticized. However, the online world was forced on the entire sector, having several effects and impacts that will be addressed herein. At this point, I want to briefly discuss the direct impact that Covid-19 has had on three groups: professors, students, and university administration.

As aforementioned, academics for their part were mostly reluctant to teach in front of a camera, either because of discomfort with the medium, or fear of making themselves redundant, or both. Now, after having been compelled to engage in online teaching, they have become acquainted with the many possibilities that digital platforms offer and also see advantages therein over live instruction. Moreover, students saw that online learning can be efficient and even convenient. These discoveries on both sides of the lectern will most likely increase the demand for online courses and degrees, probably mostly in blended formats. This will in turn intensify global competition in higher education, with many new entrants worldwide. A final group consists of universities' administrators, who most likely will use the pandemic to keep many courses online, having campaigned therefor for years without much success. Now proof exists that online courses are possible and feasible, while prepandemic, many instructors claimed the opposite, citing the aforementioned arguments.

1.3 WHAT: CHAPTERS AND CASES

Besides this introduction and the conclusion, this book consists of four main chapters, each divided into five subchapters, each of which are subdivided into five sections. The next chapter will address new instructional formats which, as aforementioned, will increasingly move into the digital sphere. Additionally, advances in artificial intelligence (AI) as well as (big) data availability will change how teaching professionals work, as well as how students will study and learn. As case study, we will look at the Georgia Institute of Technology, or Georgia Tech, considered a pioneer in the application of many such new pedagogies.

Not only instructional formats will change, but degree programs and course content will too, as will be analyzed. Higher education will increasingly move from knowledge acquisition to skills development, with a shift toward inter- and multidisciplinarity, and a steady emphasis on society's well-being and sustainability. Aalto University will serve as an example of a highly interdisciplinary approach to learning and teaching. Moreover, Aalto is also strongly committed to identifying and aiding in solving the grand societal challenges to come, some of which are already here.

Chapter 4 discusses the possibility of official degrees losing importance and more emphasis on lifelong (autonomous) learning, micro- and nanodegrees, corporate universities, and the labor market as the ultimate certification body. As a case study, we will look at Laurie Pickard, who designed her own MBA curriculum combining several MOOCs from prestigious universities around the world, costing her a fraction what an MBA program ordinarily costs.

Chapter 5 looks at changes (thus far) occurring outside of universities' core competencies. Studying is not only learning content and acquiring skills, but is also about networks and making friends. With students spending less time on university campuses, higher education will need to think of new ways to foster social activities and/or strengthen what social activities are still on campus. My own employer and institution (and alma mater), ESCP Business School, or the European School of Commerce Paris, will serve as a case study.

Chapter 6 will summarize the aforementioned and ends with a call for action for universities to respond proactively to the sector's ongoing transformations, which at least partly are leading to disruption. Too many universities still do not feel threatened by trends and phenomena that accelerated with the pandemic; even universities with strong brands might be taken by surprise in the medium to long term. Corporations such as Coca-Cola and General Electric were equally surprised when the brand equity of Apple, Google, and Amazon overtook them in value. The truth is that universities will have to fight not to lose their status and role in society. The question is: Will they do so nimbly? Or will they go kicking and screaming into the next century and beyond?

1.4 WHO: RECTOR AND RESEARCHER

I reflected for quite some time on whether this was the right place to write about myself and present my credentials, as I feared appearing egocentric and pretentious. Finally, I decided to go for it despite the discomfort, as I believe that it will help readers to understand my ideas and arguments by knowing my background.

Being a marketing and communications professor, I wrote this book from a theoretical viewpoint. Yet as a business school dean, many of my hands-on experiences enter into this work as well. In addition to marketing papers, I also have published many works on higher education, which over the years has become one of my main publication areas. My (other) principal research field is the digital world, focusing on social media and more recently on AI and its impact on business and on society at large.

In addition to research, I am also rector (sometimes dean, vice-chancellor, president, or however you want to call the position), i.e., an administrator of ESCP Business School, a cross-border, multicampus institution located variously in Berlin, London, Madrid, Paris, Turin, and Warsaw, where I have served for over 10 years in leadership positions: First as elected head of the business school's marketing department; then as administrative director of branding and communications, followed by Provost and Dean of Academic Affairs, where I was in charge of 30 degree programs and 6,000 (by now 7,000) students across our various campuses. Finally, I became the rector in charge of ESCP in Berlin, then its Dean in Paris.

Both roles – as researcher and as administrator – aided me in writing this book. For example, regarding Chapter 5, which addresses the importance of community building, my experiences heading the school's branding and communications department, alongside my theoretical knowledge of the marketing discipline, equally nurtured the text. Likewise, my insights gained from six years on the school's alumni association board worked significantly to shape my ideas.

In short, this book has been written from a particular perspective, as well as based on experiences that I have undergone. As such, readers might get the impression that it advocates for the sector's digitalization, especially the potential changes induced via advances in AI, which very well might be the case. Or, it could be biased from the perspective of a business school dean, which I don't deny. Or again, that it is written from a marketer's perspective, which would not be surprising either. Finally, readers might have the impression that this book is written from a strongly European standpoint, which, as I explain below, is also likely the case.

1.5 WHERE: EUROPE AND ELSEWHERE

As I have been based almost all my life in Europe, mainly in France and Germany, where I studied and worked for most of my career, this book is certainly written from a European standpoint. What this means is not straightforward to explain. I once characterized Europe as having "maximum cultural diversity at minimal geographical distances" (Kaplan, 2014a, p. 532) and defined a European approach to management as "a cross-cultural, societal management approach based on interdisciplinary principles" (Kaplan, 2014a, p. 529). If kept in mind, this might help readers understand some of the arguments and reasoning that they will encounter herein.

However, in order to counterbalance some of these influences and contexts, I interviewed several people from (corporate) universities and the EdTech sector, asking them each six questions related to the design and setup of the university of the twenty-first century. To that end, I interviewed, for example, Principal and Vice-Chancellor Suzanne Fortier of McGill University, Rector Grzegorz Mazurek of Kozminski

University, as well as Jean-Luc Neyraut, Deputy Director General in charge of Education, Research and Training of the Paris Region Chamber of Commerce and Industry. As my entire network is mostly Europe-based, many of my interviews were conducted with Europeans working in Europe's higher education sector. Nonetheless, I also interviewed highly interesting figures from Brazil, Canada, China, India, South Africa, and the United States. Full transcripts of some of these interviews can be found in the latter part of this book.

To conclude, I hope you enjoy this book, whose intention is to give you some ideas, perhaps even inspire. As aforementioned, all arguments herein are framed in a certain context and viewed from a certain perspective, that of a European business school rector having published quite prolifically on the subject of higher education.

2

NEW INSTRUCTIONAL APPROACHES

New instructional approaches are one of the outcomes of higher education's digital transformation, as is artificial intelligence (AI) increasingly being applied in academia. Although remote courses are not new and actually existed preinternet as "correspondence courses," the sector's transformation – even disruption – was predicted with the advent of Massive Open Online Courses (MOOCs) as well as other types of online/distance courses (Leckart, 2012). Although higher education's large-scale digitalization failed to take hold then, the pandemic gave the sector's transformation a massive impulsion, leading to strong implications for the university of the twenty-first century.

We'll begin this chapter with a short historical survey of distance learning, as well as the various types and targets of online formats. Thereafter, AI and its impact on education will be addressed, before discussing the "agony of choice" between on-site versus off-site teaching. The last section addresses digital innovations within degree programs and corresponding curricula. A simple conclusion is reached: Online teaching must make sense. Georgia Tech will serve as a case study of pioneering in new instructional approaches.

2.1 DISTANCE LEARNING: TIMES, TYPES, TARGETS

Distance learning is actually "old wine in new bottles" (Kaplan, 2014b), and while the applied medium type evolved over time, universities' reluctance to broadly use it suppressed its spread. Enter Covid-19. While online course quality certainly could have been better during the pandemic, it appeared that "bad coffee is better than no coffee." Various types of online courses exist, and, to adhere to the beverage analogy, the question had now become: "Whiskey? Or whisky?" Online learning is, however, not every student's cup of tea, not to mention that instructors able to execute it need to be well chosen. In the future, "celebrity" online educators might auction their skills for premium prices, like bottles of Dom Pérignon.

Distance Learning: Old Wine in New Bottles?

One of the earliest forays into distance education appeared in the *Boston Gazette* as early as 1728, where a stenography course in the form of weekly mailed lessons was advertised (Holmberg, 2005). This (for its time) highly innovative way of learning perfectly suited the zeitgeist of a society undergoing deep transformations preceding the Industrial Revolution. Thereafter, distance learning moved from print to the audiovisual world. Almost simultaneously, in the late 1960s/early 1970s, the UK's Open University was the first to offer short courses via television, while on the other side of the Atlantic, *Sesame Street* premiered on US public television on November 10, 1969.

Twenty years later, in 1989, the Internet was first employed for educational purposes, with the University of Phoenix offering entire online degrees on their newly launched virtual campus. So, when Dave Cormier of the Canadian University of Prince Edward Island coined the term "MOOC" in 2008, and the *New York Times* proclaimed 2012 "The Year of the MOOC" (Pappano, 2012), it could certainly be argued that distance learning is a matter of old wine in new bottles. With its advent, several voices forecasted the disruption of the higher education sector. So far, this hasn't occurred.

Covid-19: Even Bad Coffee Is Better than No Coffee at All

Covid-19 is considered a game changer with respect to distance learning. While the pandemic did not spur the wheel's reinvention with respect to online course format, an unprecedented shift in universities' mindsets took place, finally coming to terms with online instruction on a large scale. Up until then, most universities were reluctant to move their courses from live instruction to online. Covid-19 impelled an abrupt change: Corona-spurred online instruction can actually be viewed as the biggest EdTech (educational technology) experiment in modern (distance) education (Williamson, Eynon, & Potter, 2020). As far as how far and at what scale higher education will continue its engagement therewith post corona, only time will tell.

If universities do continue to massively offer online courses post corona, significant investments into infrastructure, hiring of support staff, changes in faculty compensation models, and clarifications regarding copyright issues will need to happen. During Lockdown I, online teaching was, for the most part, more improvised than really up to standard. This was obviously understandable, with universities having been taken by surprise. Professors did everything in their power to deliver quality teaching, and generally speaking, students were grateful for their efforts. It appeared that even "flawed coffee" was better than no coffee. However, in ordinary times, students most certainly expect much higher quality (Kaplan, 2020a).

MOOCs, SPOCs, SSOCs, SMOCs: Whiskey? or Whisky?

There are as many varieties of distance learning as there are flavors and spellings of Whiskey (Scots and Canadian blends) or Whisky (Irish and US brands). Like distilled malt beverages, distance learning can be categorized into four types, along two parameters: the number of students and time dependency (Kaplan & Haenlein, 2016). MOOCs are unlimited in student numbers attending classes asynchronously, i.e., they tune in to courses at their own convenience and pace. Courses that require class attendance at a specific time are referred to as SMOCs (Synchronous Mass Online Courses). SPOCs (Small Private Online Courses) are taught asynchronously, but unlike MOOCs are limited in enrollment. Courses that take place synchronously and are small are referred to as SSOCs (Synchronous Small Online Courses).

Usually the above-defined course types belong to the group of x-online courses, the "x" indicating ex-ante or structured in a preplanned sequence by a professional instructor. So-called c-online courses ("c" standing for "connectivist") do not follow a formal, predesigned curriculum, but develop as they progress. C-online instructors take on the role of facilitator with students, who make ample use of (mobile) social media (Kaplan, 2012; Kaplan & Haenlein, 2010) to work with each other as well as to develop content on their own. They decide themselves what to learn and at what time and pace, depending upon group dynamics and personal preferences.

Online Only: Not Everybody's Cup of Tea

Online learning has characteristics that render it not every student's cup of tea. To succeed, online-only learning demands a high level of self-discipline and intrinsic motivation. Usually, successful enrollees therein are older (approximately 25–30 years old) and hold previously earned traditional degrees. Accordingly, such students often seek to update or obtain skills that they directly need in their current careers. To reduce failure rates, providers apply a number of measures, which we call the 5C framework of online teaching (Kaplan & Haenlein, 2016):

Firstly, every student needs to feel the Challenge set by taking a certain course, achieved via, for example, AI-based adaptive learning methods (see next section). Secondly, the more Control students feel over their environment, the more likely their success. Control can be achieved, for example, by enabling participants to customize their own platform interfaces. Commitment to the coursework can be increased by showing participants that they are not alone but part of a larger group, for example, by providing students with an enrollee directory. Competition, for example, fostered through gamification of courses, augments enrollees' motivation to complete the course. Finally, courses should be Contemporaneous, i.e., content should refer to news and current events (Kaplan & Haenlein, 2016).

Top Teachers: Come Quick! I'm Drinking the Stars!

If distance learning isn't every student's cup of tea, it's definitely not for all instructors either. Accordingly, universities would be well advised to target instructors who are adept at teaching online. Similar to "celebrity researchers" who are courted on the job market, it appears probable that a focus on online courses will lead to "celebrity instructors," with their personal brands increasingly disconnected from those of their home institutions. Hence, universities worldwide might have to hustle so as not to miss out on these newly created star (online) teachers, recalling Dom Pérignon, French monk and originator of the eponymous Champagne, who allegedly said upon first sipping his serendipitous libation: "Come quickly! I'm drinking the stars!"

To target and identify such star instructors, the 5C framework for selecting an ideal online teacher might be of assistance (Kaplan & Haenlein, 2016). Theretoward, we've added five more Cs: To keep the (online) masses captivated, Charisma is essential. Moreover, the professor should have Competence in the academic area in which the university wants to build its brand. Course production being costly, instructors should help in your desired market positioning. Institutions should also seek Constancy, i.e., universities should avoid cultivating star teachers if the likelihood of them "defecting" to the competition is high. Compensation models must be adapted, and Contribution from further staff will be necessary, as a "star" might not want to (and should not have to) respond to potentially thousands of student queries. While good teaching assistants are a must, these might actually be AI-driven machines, as we will address in the next section.

2.2 ARTIFICIAL INTELLIGENCE: ABSOLUTELY INTRIGUING

AI, defined as "a system's ability to correctly interpret external data, to learn from such data, and to use those learnings to achieve specific goals and tasks through flexible adaptation" (Kaplan & Haenlein, 2019, 2020), has been "resident" at universities for some time now. So-called learning analytics, i.e., the results of learners' (big) data analysis, could significantly improve both professors' and students' experiences, enabling such practices as adaptive learning, wherein the speed and difficulty level optimally evolve to meet the individual learner's progress. China in particular makes ample use of AI in the higher education sector (and beyond). Looking toward the future, we can legitimately surmise whether machines and robots will replace humans in the teaching profession. Whatever the answer is, AI is indeed intriguing.

AI and Education

Several of the early advances in AI originated in a university context: The term "artificial intelligence" was coined at Dartmouth College in 1956, at a workshop organized by Stanford professor and computer scientist John McCarthy. DeepMind, a British AI company, was established by three scientists, two of them having met during their studies at University College London. DeepMind, now belonging to Google, is known for having developed AlphaGo, the first computer software that defeated a human champion in the highly complex game "Go." Consequently, we might observe that universities might actually have sowed the seeds of their own disruption with their innovation and research in the field of AI (Kaplan & Haenlein, 2019).

AI has already begun to transform higher education. Carnegie Mellon and the Technical University of Berlin are both using chatbots to respond to students' queries, thus streamlining instruction. And Georgia Tech, as we will see in our case study, has made impressive progress in this area.

Moreover, AI is also being used in research. For example, Elsevier's mother company, the British RELX Group, uses AI for the automation of academic literature review writing, thorough checks for plagiarism, or testing for potential misuse of statistics and data analysis. These tasks are of particular help in interdisciplinary research, quickly becoming the preferred approach in the university of the twenty-first century, as it requires knowledge of a variety of literature bodies, which proves complex and tedious for human researchers.

Learning Analytics

Learning analytics can be described as the measurement, collection, and analysis of (big) data about learners and their contexts, aiming at understanding and optimizing learning and teaching. More so than ever with the advent of Covid-19, many higher education institutions have discovered learning analytics and their advantages, which until then were largely unused and quietly stored on the various learning management platforms such as Blackboard or Moodle. Using learning analytics, instructors can better monitor their students' progress, understand how and by whom course resources are being used, and reflect upon their teaching style and syllabi (Baer & Carmean, 2019). What works on the course level is likewise applicable at the program or entire university level, and has the potential to hugely simplify university administrations' lives.

Furthermore, students themselves benefit from learning analytics, as these can show them their performance level, track their improvements or decline in performance, compare them to their peers, and much more. However, learning analytics also pose the question of students' right to privacy and protection. The Educause 2020 Horizon Report insists that "institutions will need to be more proactive in protecting student and employee data, and must make careful decisions around partnerships and data exchanges with other organizations, vendors, and governments" (Brown, McCormack, Reeves, Brooks, & Grajek, 2020, p. 9).

Adaptive Learning

Adaptive learning also makes use of big data, which refers to datasets characterized by "huge amounts (volume) of frequently updated data (velocity) in various formats, such as numeric, textual, or images/videos (variety)" (Kaplan & Haenlein, 2019, p. 17). Big data are considered the new machine oil in many industries and will likely be in higher education as well. Adaptive learning makes use of AI-based tools that help to fit the speed and level of instruction to the individual student (Carbonell, 1970). This tool is of particular interest regarding MOOCs, where thousands of student profiles with varying backgrounds and previous knowledge take the same course.

Adaptive learning supports student-centricity, and, therefore, lies entirely within the scope of the university of the twenty-first century. Research shows the superiority of adaptive learning methods as is shown inter alia by Alsadoon's (2020) recently conducted study: 130 students were randomly allocated to two cohorts, with one group taking a traditional course, and the other one learning academic content in adaptive learning modules. The latter cohort significantly outperformed the other cohort. Moreover, the same study suggests that activating students' relevant prior knowledge reduces the performance gap between more and less advanced learners within the adaptive learning group.

Countries and Customs and China

"Other countries, other customs" is especially apt in the case of China and its very advanced use of AI in higher education (Lynch, 2019). China demonstrates clearly where the sector could evolve to, obviously given that national data protection rights are respected. Chinese EdTech start-ups can count on state support to help them develop AI-based projects, obtaining impressive financing and funding. The EdTech start-up Squirrel AI, for example, raised more than $180 million and has exceeded $1 billion in market valuation. By now, Squirrel AI is operating in 2,000 learning centers in 200 Chinese cities, with more than one million students in its database (Hao, 2019).

But China goes beyond this. Xian University, for example, installed facial recognition cameras and AI-driven gates as a part of the Education Ministry's smart campuses campaign. Students need to pass face scanners to enter the library, buildings, or register attendance. Cameras furthermore are used to analyze the behavior of faculty and students, and to keep an eye on students' attentiveness. The cameras can even recognize seven emotions in subjects: anger, disappointment, happiness, neutral, sadness, fear, and surprise. Furthermore, Guanyu Technology supplies chip-fitted "smart uniforms" in the southwestern province of Guizhou to track students' locations. Such surveillance naturally raises privacy and data protection concerns for educators, students, and their parents (Roberts et al., 2020).

Humans versus Machines I

China's extensive use of AI has a further objective: overcoming its shortage of (quality) teachers, potentially supplementing or even replacing them in order to train their millions of students nationwide. Presently, AI is mainly used to free up faculty from paperwork, time which they can put toward higher-value activities. So while humans are still needed, in the future, we might be justified in asking whether human instructors will be replaced by machines altogether.

Whatever the case, what is certain is that faculty will have to change the way they teach, making ample use of all available data and analytics. AI will simplify instructors' lives, eliminating in a very efficient way such tedious activities as replying to ever-recurring questions repeatedly. Grading will be outsourced to machines, as has already been done for multiple-choice exams for quite some time. Modern AI is also able to evaluate exam papers and student essays. Actually, AI-driven machines can imitate a professor's grading pattern within only one percentage point divergence, thus freeing up instructors not only to act as coaches and facilitators during class but also to engage in research (Zawacki-Richter, Marín, Bond, & Gouverneur, 2019).

2.3 AGONY OF CHOICE: ON-SITE VERSUS OFF-SITE

With courses increasingly moving online, students might ask why they should come to campus at all. Pure (theoretical) content sessions will likely be taught remotely, with on-campus instruction focused on active, experiential learning, case-study presentations, or group work. If successful, this would lead to the much-discussed and much-tried flipped classroom, so far with mixed results where it has been tried. Alongside the aforementioned "celeb" online instructors, it will be incumbent upon the rest of the faculty to evolve from (pure) knowledge providers to coaches and facilitators, building upon what students have previously learned online. One might ask the (utopic, for now) question if such coaching and facilitation could also be executed by AI-driven robots and machines both online and offline, replacing human instructors for good. A look below at Britney Spears and the music industry's digital transformation might give us some insight therein. But first, we'll ask the following ultimate question.

Why Come to Campus?

A legitimate question is why students should come to campus at all, with more and more courses moving online. If on-site lectures are given frontally, without notable discussions and exchanges, students will feel as though going to campus is a waste of their time, as online sessions definitely offer the advantage of being able to stay in bed longer. However, motivating students to spend time on campus is, as we will see in chapter 5, critical in forging their attachment to their school. In-class debates and dialogs, team projects, and case presentations all provide reasons to enter the university buildings. Accordingly, universities' physical plants must be inviting to welcome such live interaction.

Not only students, but professors too will need convincing that being on campus is in their interest. Since universities' shutdowns compelled by Covid-19, many faculty members experienced the advantage of working from home, causing many of them to question whether they need to be on campus. Effective community building, however, demands the presence of the various stakeholders. The introduction of (physical) office hours might do the trick, though they certainly won't be easy to enforce. Providing faculty with workspaces including all of the amenities alongside an inviting ambience inside buildings and on campus could draw them back to campus.

Flipped Classroom: Final Chance

Higher education's digital transformation might finally result in the flipped classroom, where students are asked to prepare in advance by learning theories, concepts, and the like before attending class (Bowen, 2013), enabling professors to focus on in-depth instruction and skills development during class sessions. Several other advantages exist to the flipped classroom, such as enabling students to study on their own schedule and at their own pace, preparing questions at home, encouraging them to think outside the box, or simply training them in autonomous learning, which will become increasingly important (cf. Chapter 4).

The flipped classroom is not really a new approach. For the entire history of education, instructors have tried to get their students to prepare for class, with mixed success (Jarvis, 2020). However, there is a (final) chance that more engaging visuals and the online environment might be more appealing than a textbook. Also, learning analytics show whether a student actually attended the online session, thereby enabling professors to see students' progress. Quizzes during the online sessions could make learning fun, as well as serve as motivators for students to delve into the content made available digitally.

Teachers as Coaches and Facilitators

As aforementioned, the online sphere with its MOOCs and SMOCs will most likely produce high-profile instructors teaching thousands of students worldwide. This might prompt us to ask what role the rest of the faculty has in such a scenario. The answer is that they will increasingly become facilitators and coaches, putting into perspective what students learn online and training them using hands-on exercises, group work, in-class discussions, and so forth. While this might feel like demotion to some faculty members, we should look at it from a positive angle: What professor actually enjoys teaching the same theories and concepts over and over again, several times a year, over decades? By outsourcing this content to online teachers, the others are free to focus on the job's fun part: discussions with students, critically analyzing content, and ultimately learning from each other.

This means that those complementary online instructors cannot afford to be boring and dry, lest they find themselves replaced by the future generation of AI machines, as we will see in the next section. Instructors of the twenty-first century will definitely need to bring it all together: the online and the on-site. Actually, they will need to be and become entertainers, such as you'd find in a Club Med resort or on a Carnival Cruise.

Humans versus Machines II

It might sound utopian – and perhaps it is – but AI progress indicates that some time in the future, robots will be able to perfectly read students' emotions and engage with them in conversations, to mention just two possible areas where AI-driven machines might replace human instructors (Kaplan & Haenlein, 2019). AI-driven robots might even be less costly than salaried professors, which would render the machine a quite interesting alternative for universities across the globe that are struggling: definitely another reason why we humans should be vigilant.

Only time will tell if this prediction becomes reality. Ultimately, the real question will be whether students prefer human instructors or AI-driven machines as their educators.

The answer might not be as straightforward as you think (or hope). In this context, a recent study by Spanish IE University's Center for the Governance of Change showed that 25% of Europeans would actually rather that politics were conducted by AI and not by human politicians, who as we are only too aware, are often corrupt or ideologically extreme (Rubio et al., 2019).

Britney Spears as Prime Example?

Within the human vs machine discussion, there might be some light at the end of the tunnel. In order to make the point here, it will be necessary, however, to take an even bolder approach, claiming that future professors should take as their example international pop icon Britney Spears (as promised above). The author also admits to being fan of Spears since the beginning of her career, and therefore whenever possible, will bring her into the conversation (Kaplan & Haenlein, 2012). Regardless, and although not straightforward, the analogy of a professor and the higher education sector and an international recording artist and the music industry makes sense...at least to this book's author.

Regarding the music industry, although traditional compact discs (CDs) (not to mention audiocassettes) were replaced by mp3s long ago, live concerts still exist, possibly even having increased in numbers and importance. Watching Britney Spears, Justin Bieber, or Cardi B perform live will most likely remain the more exciting experience compared to listening to their music on one's device or watching their YouTube channels or TikTok videos. Similarly, this will be the case for online modules vs. live courses; it will still be more exciting to see the professor at the front of the lecture hall than it will to watch a hologram of him or her. Obviously, this only holds true if the respective professor has a certain degree of star appeal…as does pop princess Britney (Kaplan & Haenlein, 2016).

2.4 DIGITAL INNOVATION: FROM COURSES TO CURRICULA

Since corona, everybody knows that online and offline courses each have their advantages and drawbacks. Going forward, cases will be rare where it makes sense to offer an entire program on-site only. The same applies to purely online programs, although there are more justifications for an online-only than for a fully offline curriculum. Moreover, universities should avoid other sectors' errors and understand that going online is not simply transferring an offline program into the virtual sphere. To exploit the online world to its fullest, pedagogical innovations and changes in program structure are in order. Or, to put it even more simply, moving a course and curriculum online must simply make sense!

100% Offline: Yes, but…

We will start with the most obvious case, i.e., programs that are delivered 100% on-site, that is, offline with no notable online elements integrated. This has been the case for the huge majority of study programs at higher education institutions worldwide – until Covid-19 suddenly arrived and shook up the sector. The educational world changed, and universities and administrators began to rethink and conceive of what actually might make sense in terms of online teaching going forward, post corona.

It will be difficult to go back to teaching offline only. Even after much reflection, it is hard to imagine any situation or context where it might make sense to have a university program that takes place entirely on-site with no online elements. Students will always have to learn some hard facts and theories within their study areas. Such pure knowledge seems to be better transmitted via well-designed online modules as opposed to repeated courses in the lecture hall. The only case wherein a 100% offline program might be sensible is if the market would consider it as signal of extremely high-quality teaching. This, however, appears increasingly unlikely. Therefore we, for now, would rather turn the "Yes, but" into a clear "No, never."

100% Online: Yes, but...

More and more online-only study programs are seeing the light of day. Such programs, however, might lose out in several aspects. Studying is more than just learning material and new knowledge. The exchange among students in class, and even more so outside the lecture hall accompanied by a beer or a cup of coffee, is worth mention. While you can imitate offline group sessions in online breakout rooms, the drinking part is definitely more difficult to mimic. During lockdown, we all experienced the Zoom gatherings with friends and family being not nearly as satisfying as the live version.

Yet, in contrast to 100% offline, there are several scenarios where 100% online programs make sense: When, for example, participants are just not able to get to campus, having a long commute that is seasonally made difficult by weather; caring for children or ill or disabled family members, unable to afford airfare or living costs, or simply reluctant to travel for health reasons. Finally, purely online courses might also work for learners interested only in the study content or the degree itself, or in the latter case not even caring about content altogether. While this might justify 100% online programs from a student perspective, it's more fraught from the university's perspective. Clearly not all material is teachable to the same degree online as offline; so ultimately, it's a question of quality.

The Right Mix: Yes, Please...

These trade-offs between online and offline lead to the conclusion that programs at the university of the twenty-first century will most likely all pursue a blended approach with a mix of both environments. In addition, for example, online elements might also increase program quality, in that they allow for modules taught by other institutions' "guest star" professors or even relevant personalities outside academia, for whom it is often difficult to block out an entire day for traveling to a destination. However, it might be easier to persuade them to take an hour out of their busy schedules to give a short presentation online.

Further reflection regarding finding the right mix underscores the fact that distinct academic areas will demand differing balances of offline and online modules. Becoming a chemist or a biologist might require several hours a day in laboratories. Likewise, degrees in the creative arts might demand more offline training than would, for example, business administration. A university's senior administration should accordingly allow a lot of flexibility when it comes to identifying the right balance for a given program.

200% of Innovation Potential

Several sectors and industries have made the error of simply replicating their offline environments on online platforms. By now, we know that this is not an optimum strategy, and higher education should avoid going down this road. Pedagogical innovation will become key in differentiating a university from the competition, as all higher education institutions move an increasing number of courses online (Kaplan, 2018a). Accordingly, only via true pedagogical innovation as opposed to minor tweaks at the margins, can universities properly exploit the online sphere's potential (Thibierge, 2020).

To give an example of such innovations enabled via the digital sphere only, one can imagine entire new structures and setups of programs. Let's say that during a four-year curriculum, during their first year, students work part-time at a company or other organization while simultaneously following online modules to acquire relevant general theories and concepts. You might add some on-site sessions scheduled for when students are not working for their employer. Years two and three then would be spent entirely on-site, "spiked" with some online elements. During this long-term period on campus, focus could be on discussions, exchanges, networking, and live presentations. Finally, the fourth and last study year, students could return to their companies and organizations, again working part-time, but still benefitting from online tutoring and coaching, personal development sessions, and so forth.

1,000% Simply Put: Online Must Make Sense!

By now, we should all agree that online teaching is not the ideal format for all subjects, all courses, and all situations. In many cases, offline is and will be the better solution. However, in particular during the present pandemic, several university presidents have proclaimed, almost solemnly, that in the future a certain minimum ratio of courses at their institutions should remain only online, across the board and without exception. This would be a mistake and is so key that this section's headline just as solemnly declares: 1,000% simply put: Online must make sense.

The virtual sphere provides several very precise possibilities that the offline environment does not, and this needs to be the mindset. For example, the digital environment enables fostering a sense of proximity (Mucharraz & Venuti, 2020) when students are actually distant from their institutions. This might be useful during foreign study exchanges at distant partner institutions when universities ordinarily lose contact with their students. The same applies to students usually not coming to campus during internship periods, however spending lots of hours online...

2.5 HIGH TECH: GEORGIA TECH

As its name indicates, the Georgia Institute of Technology, commonly referred to as Georgia Tech, serves as prime example of a university that makes ample use of technological advances and the digital sphere for instruction. As early as 2013, Georgia Tech began offering its MSc in Computer Science also in a 100% online option. The same program gave birth to probably the best-known AI-based teaching assistant, Jill Watson, who responds to thousands of students without their being aware that they're conversing with a machine, not a human. Moreover, Georgia Tech showed its pioneering spirit once more by creating an entire STEM training and coaching space on the virtual platform Second Life. Finally, also during lockdown, Georgia Tech was one of the first to publicly state how the pandemic will impact the university's (digital) strategy of the future.

Georgia Tech's Pioneering Role in Online Education

Georgia Tech is one of the top-ranked public universities in the United States, mainly based in Atlanta, Georgia. It currently enrolls over 30,000 students, as well as approximately 6,000 and 2,000 administrative and academic staff, respectively. Established in 1885, with the aim of reconstructing and building an industry-based economy after the US Civil War, innovation and openness to change lies within the university's DNA since its founding. Combined with its focus on science and technology, this makes it an ideal candidate for pioneering and advancing online education.

This pioneer spirit has led to several awards and recognition for Georgia Tech. For example, the university's fully online computer science master's degree has become one of the most successful online programs in recruiting students, according to the 2018 report of the Observatory on Borderless Higher Education (OBHE). In 2019, the same master's program was presented the Gold Award by the Reimagine Education Conference for nurturing 21st-century skills. Georgia Tech is constantly working on being at the forefront of innovative education. By creating its Center for 21st Century Universities, its living laboratory for fundamental change in education, Georgia Tech is "committed to leading the initiatives that will define the next generation of educational practices and technologies," as described on its website. To motivate faculty to lead on the online path, Georgia Tech awards a $3,000 Teaching Excellence Award for Online Teaching to one of its full-time professors annually.

Georgia Tech's OMSCS

As aforementioned, one of Georgia Tech's online successes is its Master of Science in Computer Science (OMSCS), taught entirely via MOOCs. It all began with a simple idea: Use technology to render education at a top university more accessible to more people. In partnership with AT&T and Udacity, this idea became reality as of 2013. OMSCS began with under 400 students enrolled, and today it enrolls 10,000 students from nearly 120 countries, with nearly 30,000 applicants.

At approximately $7,000, OMSCS tuition is far below that of the on-campus version. Despite this, Georgia Tech decided to not indicate the program's online nature on the students' diplomas and transcripts, delivering the same diploma as its on-site version. While other universities are often reluctant to offer online programs at lower cost than their offline ones for fear of cannibalization, Georgia Tech correctly embraced another vision: Goodman, Melkers, and Pallais (2019) used the OMSCS as prime example of the combination of "the inexpensive nature of online education with a highly regarded degree program," and empirically showed that the establishment of the program's online version significantly increased overall enrollment, and did not lead to the much-feared bogeyman of substitution. Moreover, Barack Obama (2015) cited OMSCS as a much-needed innovation on the educational landscape to counter the issue of higher education's increasing cost.

Georgia Tech's Jill Watson

Georgia Tech's OMSCS birthed another innovation in the digital environment: the world's probably best-known artificially intelligent teaching assistant (TA), Jill Watson. This AI-based TA was built on IBM's Watson platform and developed by Ashok Goel, professor of interactive computing, who introduced the virtual TA into his course on Knowledge-Based Artificial Intelligence – Cognitive Systems.

The reasons for Jill's introduction were twofold: Firstly, the small (human) team around Ashok Goel was not able to respond to the approximately 10,000 student queries per semester; and secondly, the aim of the virtual TA was also to increase student engagement; Professor Goel was afraid of losing many of his students over the course of the term, similarly to what occurred in other MOOCs. Jill Watson responds to routine questions such as the course's office hours, i.e., questions that have a straightforward, clear answer; and human teaching assistants jump in for more complex queries. The results are so convincing, with Jill responding correctly to 97% of the queries, that most of the students were not aware that they were chatting with a virtual AI-based teaching assistant (Todd, 2017).

Georgia Tech's Second Life

Another example of Georgia Tech's trailblazing is its use of the virtual social world Second Life (Kaplan & Haenlein, 2009a, b). As early as 2011, the university announced that it

> *...would create and oversee a STEM training program hosted in the Second Life virtual world where disabled students would create avatars and receive free help from educators and experts in every STEM field.*
>
> (Carter, 2011)

On the virtual island, students in the form of their avatars find classrooms, cafes and lounges, spaces for tutoring, and so forth. They interact with their mentors, attend lectures, conduct experiments, or learn STEM subjects by, just to give one example, going on a virtual scavenger hunt.

The project's aim was to find students interested in career in the STEM fields, who, without mentoring, would most likely not pursue such a path as a result of their disability. By now, several students who participated in the Second Life mentoring program have already begun careers in one of the STEM areas. Nonetheless, while the Second Life island was the original focus of the mentoring program, the connecting modes between students and mentors have moved to other platforms such as WhatsApp and the like over the program's duration, leading to the island's desertion.

Georgia Tech's Post-Covid-19 Future

Doubtless, it is highly interesting to see how a pioneer in online education itself forecasts the post-Covid-19 era. A look at the university's report, "Deliberate Innovation, Lifetime Education," which summarizes the collective work and reflections of more than 50 faculty, staff, and students, shows Georgia Tech's plans for the future: Commitment to lifelong learning, the application of technology to scale and improve learners' services, as well as further expanding beyond Atlanta.

One project in the works is to eliminate all on-site lectures enrolling more than 70, redesigning them, and moving them to the online sphere. On-campus teaching would follow the aforementioned flipped classroom model. Also, assessments of course content would move online. The role of teaching assistants would be taken over by AI, as stated in Georgia Tech's report. While extending its programs delivered 100% online and affordably priced, the university adheres to on-site teaching, totally aware that needs with respect to classroom space will change. Lecture halls and auditoriums will be replaced by small and medium-sized spaces with adaptable classroom configuration. Office space will decrease, as will the number of dormitory rooms proportional to student numbers. Partnering with industry players in the high-tech sector is also viewed as necessary to the university's future plans. Thus, Georgia Tech is a model of the university of the twenty-first century.

3

FROM KNOWLEDGE ACQUISITION TO (SOCIETAL) SKILLS DEVELOPMENT

Not only do instructional formats change, but the university of the twenty-first century will also need to increasingly move from focusing on knowledge acquisition to the development of (societal) skills. Society's digitalization and advances in artificial intelligence (AI) will have a strong impact on the economy, job markets, and corresponding rapidly changing job requirements, in response to which employees will constantly have to adapt to dynamic realities. In addition to digitalization, the main challenges of today's society, for example global warming, show that solutions can no longer be sought in a single academic area, but rather necessitate collaboration between disciplines (Gibbons et al., 1994). Again, this was brought to the fore with the pandemic having brought entire economies grinding to a halt. These challenges prove beyond a doubt that universities need to continue and even intensify students' mastery of societal skills and development of sustainable mindsets.

This chapter's opening section will give insights into how higher education can increase students' adaptability and autonomous learning ability. Following that, advantages and challenges of a multi- and interdisciplinary approach to teaching will be discussed. The third section addresses students' expectations of the university of the twenty-first century to teach them responsible leadership and how academia can support their quest. Not only will universities need to teach ethics, societal responsibility, and sustainability, but they also will be required to walk the walk, which is the topic of this chapter's fourth part. Aalto University, with its slogan "Toward a Better World," heavily applies a multi- and interdisciplinary approach to learning and teaching, and will stand as the case study in this chapter's final section.

3.1 AUTONOMOUS AND ADAPTABLE

Job requirements and necessary knowledge are evolving at the speed of mobile phone upgrades. Change appears to indeed be the only constant in future professional lives, rendering adaptability and autonomy the name of the game. Such skills can be conferred by delivering students more breadth than depth. Mastering a given field's basic lexicon as well as its skeleton, students will be enabled to acquire more detailed knowledge on their own. Courses and degree programs should expose learners to variations and teach them creativity and agility. Mandatory study abroad, and internships foster contextual change. Finally, applicants for a given program should already be selected for their adaptive capacity and autonomous learning aptitude, not forgetting alumni mentoring them and welcoming them into their networks. Aside, the attentive reader will remark that on the occasion and to create some change, this subchapter is divided in only four, not five, subsections…

More Breadth, Less Depth

When schools were first established, access to knowledge was a privilege, so much so that the lucky few who were allowed to learn considered school a leisure-time pursuit. This can be seen in the etymology of "school," which derives from the Greek σχολή [scholē] and means "leisure" and "that in which leisure is employed." Over the centuries, of course, knowledge became accessible to the broad public. Today, we carry virtually all knowledge literally in our pockets, on our devices. Knowledge is available to everyone instantly and at low cost compared to its cost in the past (Kaplan & Haenlein, 2016).

Such abundance of knowledge renders knowing several disciplines and their interlinkages as an advantage, favoring breadth over knowing every detail of a single discipline. Lest the reader misunderstand; while deep knowledge is of course valuable and it would be ideal if students knew numerous subjects in depth, this is unrealistic. Because we can't give most students both; it is preferable that they know something of many disciplines. This will impel students to obtain more precise expertise on their own, which they will be motivated to do as employment opportunities arise. Instructors accordingly should help students to acquire skills that enable them to understand basic structures of several disciplines, acquire more precise, in-depth knowledge on their own, and make the connections therebetween. Disciplinary boundaries are already being challenged as never before due to the sheer quantity of information and knowledge that we humans have amassed.

Change and Creativity

Students need to face and adjust to change, rapidly and recurrently. One way to teach them such flexibility and adaptability is to incorporate entrepreneurship, innovation, and creativity into every curriculum, wherein students learn the (theoretical) basics about change and develop an entrepreneurial, hands-on mindset. Regarding future contextual diversity, universities must motivate students to strive for innovation, out-of-the-box thinking, and to consider inevitable failures as setups (to borrow a volleyball term) for potential success – one of the marks of a successful entrepreneur. Innovation and creativity are the all-terrain vehicles in the topography of constant change and a prerequisite for survival in today's job markets and those of the future.

Actually, adaptability can be taught in any course by deliberately creating situations of change. An example might be something as simple as integrating a group project into a course and then changing its parameters over the course of the semester. The instructor could even advance the deadline by one week. Students won't like it, but if the instructor explains the logic behind such "curve balls," they will not only understand it, but perhaps even appreciate it. We can also bring students from vastly different academic fields together and have them work in teams. Thusly, they will experience how other fields speak differing languages, which should also increase flexibility and openness. In brief, students should be pushed outside their comfort zones as much as possible toward increasing their adaptability and flexibility.

Multicountry and Multijob

We all know that moving to another country or starting a new job or internship increases one's adaptivity. As such, students need to encounter new ways of thinking and working, whether about a new country or a new organizational culture. Accordingly, the university of the twenty-first century should integrate a mandatory residency at a partner university in another country, whether for a semester or an entire year, an internship, or a six-week mini course. Curricula must leave room for such residencies and themselves to integrate a certain degree of flexibility; if a student desires a gap year to study, volunteer, or work abroad, or have an intensive experience with an employer, every effort should be made to enable this.

Later on, the point will be elaborated upon that higher education institutions need to consider students as clients (in nonacademic matters) and provide them with "concierge service" (cf. Chapter 5). On the other hand, universities must not deprive students of valuable learning opportunities by being too accommodating. Thus, having to seek internships on their own or to arrange their own housing during a residency abroad will naturally increase students' flexibility, resilience, and life experience. Again, while students will not be happy with universities not making such arrangements for them, if we explain to them the reasoning behind such policies, not only might it motivate them to take on these challenges, but when they score that internship or find that housing, their confidence will soar.

Admissions and Alumni

A further implication of skills becoming more important than learning in depth and by heart is that students should be admitted to programs not (only) based on their scholastic achievements. Applicants' flexibility and autonomous learning capabilities should be taken into account in the admissions process. While skills can obviously be taught, universities should provide the job market with the most qualified graduates; the higher their starting point in necessary skills for their future employer, the better the final result at graduation will be. This means that areas such as leadership potential, aptitude for teamwork, and adaptability should be looked at by admissions personnel.

Regarding alumni, too, universities need to rethink and adapt. Upskilling and reskilling options should be provided by one's alma mater, which should welcome alumni back as clients of lifelong learning offerings. Ironically, if you train your students "too well" in autonomous learning, it renders their return unnecessary. Therefore, universities might be tempted not to hone students' autonomy for fear that this would eliminate demand for (highly profitable) executive education courses. However, deliberate withholding would be unethical, and as will be addressed below, we have high expectations of universities being ethical and accountable. Nonetheless, options such as a subscription-based system of lifelong learning courses could be implemented to avoiding such ethical dilemmas or conflicts of interest.

3.2 MULTISKILLED AND MULTIDISCIPLINED

The university of the twenty-first century should foster multi- and interdisciplinarity, as today's societal challenges require global solutions that go beyond a single discipline. By doing so, students' critical thinking skills will be sharpened, enabling them to think outside the box, which is necessary to solving complex problems and which learning quantities of material by heart will not achieve. As a minimum, each student, independently of his or her study area(s), should acquire a sound understanding of the digital transformation that is currently occurring, as well as its consequences for society at large. To enable such multi- and interdisciplinarity, universities will need to evolve their internal structures, i.e., academic departments and faculties.

From Local to Global

As early as 2008, the Tokyo G8 university summit cited universities' critical task as "training leaders with the skills to solve regional and local problems from a global and interdisciplinary perspective," as most of our hardest-to-resolve problems necessitate an interdisciplinary approach to tackle them. The pandemic recently demonstrated this on a formidable level; to address this crisis, science, economics, psychology, public policy, culture, and several other academic areas had to coordinate. Advances in AI, big data, and the Internet-of-things demonstrate the same need vis-a-vis interdisciplinarity. To give another example, global warming and climate change demand the interlinkage of a number of disciplines (Snow, 1963).

Multi- and interdisciplinarity cultivate the ability to approach problems from a broad, global perspective. Students begin to think outside the box, drawing from a range of concepts, disciplines, and perspectives to identify the best integrated solutions to the world's multifaceted problems. It has been proven that students who are taught from a multi- and interdisciplinary approach are better at applying their knowledge of one discipline to another, and in turn gain a better, deeper learning experience (Kaplan, 2018a). Moreover, research has shown that highly creative and innovative people are able to make links between differing areas of study, schools of thought, and disciplines (Robinson, 2011).

From Trivial to Critical

Until now, higher education has placed inordinate weight on rote learning of theories and concepts, which, as aforementioned, we now carry on our persons in our mobile devices.

Accordingly, it is vital for students to learn the basics of several disciplines toward being able to locate relevant knowledge independently and being able to learn it quickly when needed. Important enough to be stressed once again, it would obviously be ideal for us all to know everything in detail, but in the standard three-or-four-year program, this isn't realistic.

Instead of students learning material by heart, universities need to develop students' analytical, questioning, and above all critical thinking skills, all sorely needed in the labor market. Such critical thinking is cultivated by multi- and inter-disciplinarity, as it enables students to go beyond one discipline or major, and consider further approaches and disciplines (Davis, 1997), learning to compare and contrast a given issue from a variety of angles.

From Analog to Digital

One of the key challenges of the twenty-first century, alongside sustainability, is society's digital transformation, which clearly has an impact on academic content and curricula. Above all, human beings will have to accept that machines, at least to a certain degree, will constitute some portion of their future coworker cohort. Therefore, all humans must acquire at least a minimum comprehension of coding and a coding language. The idea here is not to achieve expert level, but rather, just as knowing some basic Russian is useful when collaborating with Russia, learning the basics of programming will result in human employees better understanding their robotic, AI-driven team members.

Machines will probably outperform humans in a major portion of analytical tasks. Such a phenomenon renders training in soft skills (Huang & Rust, 2018), such as teamwork and listening, of particular importance. It is therein that humans most likely will continue to outperform AI, at least in the medium term. Many professions will become obsolete, rendering an ethical approach to technological progress crucial. Accordingly, some contend that higher education should broadly integrate courses treating AI and humanity concomitantly (Keating & Nourbakhsh, 2018). Efficient twenty-first century education must be predicated on the human–machine interface. Yet, such a development will not only lead to the disappearance of jobs, but also of many courses and subjects, which might in turn lead to quarrels and tension among faculty.

From Solely to Jointly

Universities are currently structured hierarchically by faculties and academic departments, constituting a barrier to interdisciplinary teaching, and for that matter, research (Boden & Borrego, 2011). Consequently, academics struggle to push boundaries of content and methods that go beyond the departmental structure. As an initial response, higher education institutions must establish multi- and interdisciplinary research centers in addition to academic departments. While such centers foster research cooperation between faculty members coming from differing disciplines, this might not be sufficient with respect to teaching. The university of the twenty-first century needs to shift from a vertical structure to horizontal cooperation, at all levels.

However, the dissolution of departmental structures might not be enough to foster a multi- and interdisciplinary approach. For example, there are very few interdisciplinary journals, making it difficult for researchers to pass the double-blind review process and eventually get published. A professor's career trajectory, and in some cases his or her compensation, depend upon research output. Current policies will have to be revised to enable evaluating the quality rather than the quantity of faculty members' publications. Such a shift most certainly will be met by resistance from some faculty members, at least those who are successful in the current environment, with ensuing hot debates on the horizon. We might need to start small with some beta tests; we also might recognize and promote professors who are keen on working in an interdisciplinary setting. While change might take time, it might be well worth it.

—

Again four instead of five subsections. *Change again it is…*

3.3 SOCIETAL AND SUSTAINABLE

As mentioned in the introduction, one of the universities' three missions is public service. Students increasingly ask academia to teach them content and skills from a standpoint that will help them make a positive impact on societal challenges such as diversity, poverty, and sustainability. Not only should ethics content be part of every program's curriculum, but likewise, all courses should seek to cultivate an ethics mindset. As ethics-related content might be culture-dependent and addressed differently across the globe, such modules must be sensitively designed. Universities will not only need to obtain professors' buy-in to evolve their courses accordingly, but will also need to add this element into their research activities, which optimally would in turn generate ways to positively influence today's main global challenges. Finally, students want to see universities applying such principles, for example, fostering a diverse student enrollment (Kaplan, 2020b).

Society and Education

Education has always been considered a public good, its purpose being to contribute to society's welfare (Council of the European Union, 2014), and, thus, its societal nature is one of its main characteristics (Nedbalová, Greenacre, & Schulz, 2014). Higher education should accordingly educate responsible and accountable leaders in their respective domains. However, universities' quests for revenue and reputation have led them to sideline or even neglect their stated societal purpose. While it is certainly true that a reduction in funding with simultaneously increasing costs impels universities to run as businesses (Friga, Bettis, & Sullivan, 2003), it is concomitantly the case that businesses are increasingly called upon to act for the good of society at large instead of only increasing shareholder value. Consistent with Sustainable Development Goal #4, Quality Education, the university of the twenty-first century must refocus on its primarily societal purpose.

Furthermore, students themselves expect societal purpose to be integrated into their programs. They understand that there is no purpose in earning high salaries and owning a penthouse if a global warming–induced tornado tears it to shreds. The student-led Fridays for future movement are further proof of this understanding. If you incorporate sustainability into their existing curriculum, students will ask for an entire course dedicated thereto. Integrating an elective on sustainability will lead to students demanding that it be required for all students. Ultimately, they will demand an entire degree in sustainability, which can only be a good thing.

Ethics and Curricula

Faculties and department heads often discuss whether curricula should include a dedicated course on ethics, or if modules on ethics should be part of every course (Callahan, 1980). Universities should do both; if there is no dedicated ethics course, it appears as if the subject is not of equal importance to the other courses in the curriculum. However, one course on ethics is not enough. In addition thereto, each professor should integrate ethics questions and discussions into all of their courses. Imagine a finance professor never mentioning ethics or a law professor never addressing an attorney's ethical responsibilities. Such inconsistency would render a dedicated ethics course a farce.

Accordingly, the university of the twenty-first century must ask whether curricula and courses across the board address subjects from a societal and sustainable perspective. Do business students learn about responsible and ethical management? Do engineering students learn how to construct a carbon-neutral building or a bridge that won't collapse? Are data scientists well aware of data protection rights, and at the same time of the consequences of too many privacy restrictions on a country's economy and employment market? The guiding word here is "integrity."

Culture and Plagiarism

The university of the twenty-first century increasingly has a diverse student body in terms of socioeconomic backgrounds, previous studies, and ethnocultural profiles. Ethics and cultures are an important topic in this respect, as the concept "societal" will not be interpreted universally. European management is, by definition, societal (not that other regions do not pursue societal aspects), for historical reasons that can be theoretically traced (Kaplan, 2014a). Universities need to be sensitive thereto and clearly understand any cultural differences therein.

One example thereof is plagiarism. While it seems straightforward to define plagiarism, experience shows that it is not interpreted the same way in China, for example, as it is in Germany. Asian countries, or so-called collectivist cultures, prioritize the needs of the community over those of the individual. Therefore, ideas that are helpful to an entire group are ultimately considered universal knowledge. Students growing up in such cultures, therefore, might not comprehend the Western importance attached to quotations and citations. On the contrary, they even might feel discomfort in putting the individual above the group. Therefore, rules need to be clearly and explicitly communicated and explained, obviously in a sensitive way (Bloch, 2008).

Professors and Impact

Precisely because academic freedom is a key tenet of higher education, not every faculty member will agree to integrate ethics, sustainability, and societal welfare into his or her courses. Therefore, universities need buy-in from professors, which for the majority of them will not be a problem. To incentivize them, faculty members who prominently integrate ethics content into their courses might be publicized, showcased, or otherwise recognized. Universities might also query students in course evaluations as to whether they are pleased with the ethics aspects of a given course. This, in turn, might serve as a reminder to faculty that these topics should be part of their courses. However, such moves must be discussed and agreed upon by the entire faculty.

A more complicated issue is that of professors' research nurturing their teaching. Should a professor be encouraged to research only subjects with immediate or direct societal benefit? This question in itself will quickly become ideological in nature when taking into account the mantra of academic freedom and a faculty member's being able to study whatever topic she/he desires. Also related to research, we might ask whether the university of the twenty-first century has an obligation to disseminate its faculty's research to the broader public as opposed to "guarding it" in academic journals, usually read only by other academics (de Jong, Smit, & van Drooge, 2016).

Inclusion and Diversity

As aforementioned, universities need to walk the talk when it comes to diversity. To anticipate doing so, the higher education institution of the twenty-first century should not only admit minority members, it must also actively foster diversity among its students. The same applies to faculty, staff, and administration. It's not sufficient to recruit students and hire faculty from diverse backgrounds; integrating them into the university community is essential (Tienda, 2013).

In this section, we'll focus on the student population regarding inclusion. Universities, especially those that are highly selective, must rethink their recruiting and admissions. While providing financial aid to applicants from socially weaker backgrounds is definitely a must, higher education could go further. Instead of looking at applicants' scholastic performance only, universities should also extend opportunities to applicants whose scholastic performance is below par, but who nevertheless show high potential through other means when coming from difficult life situations. And, when such applicants are accepted, it is incumbent upon the institution to ensure that these students are not treated as outcasts, but rather are welcomed. This is easier said than done and will certainly require effort on the institution's part such as strengthening their Diversity and Inclusion Division, or, if not yet existing, opening such a department (Haring-Smith, 2012). High-potential students from a variety of backgrounds are needed to enable a positive societal and social transition to the university of the twenty-first century. Accordingly, universities must do their part in improving society at large.

3.4 WALKING THE TALK

Beyond course and program content, universities will be held accountable for walking the talk. Teaching sustainability and societal skills will not be enough. Students and other stakeholders want universities to practice what they preach, i.e., operate sustainable and ever ecofriendlier physical plants. Campus canteens and cafeterias providing (only) sustainable food options is most often the most tangible manifestation of "greenness." Walking the talk will help universities in their rankings, increasing the value of "green" behavior. However, to be consistent, the university of the twenty-first century will also need to act responsibly even when doing so might harm its rankings, as will be explained further below. Finally, universities are expected to take strong stances on societal welfare and their administrations to lead by example.

Campus: Green and Greener

Students want their universities to "act green," and are the driving force therebehind. In 2016, the "Principles for Responsible Management Education" (PRME) initiative, sponsored by the United Nations, surveyed nearly 2,000 students worldwide. The results showed that, compared to previous ones, recent student intakes are more willing to sacrifice part of their future (hypothetical) income if their employers are active in environmental protection. And incidentally: once you start going green, the great thing is that it's impossible to go backwards, as students continuously challenge us to "go even greener." They'll scrutinize their university and whether or not it's walking the talk, i.e., Are buildings energy efficient? Are operations sustainable? Is waste separated and sent for recycling? (Sobczak & Mukhi, 2016).

Likewise, students will demand that their campus life and student societies (see chapter 5) engage in sustainable behavior, supported and encouraged by their institutions. A welcome initiative of the university of the twenty-first century is the establishment of a green office, i.e., an entity funded by the institution, managed by students and staff together, with the objective of connecting, informing, and supporting the university and its stakeholders to act sustainably in all dimensions and operations (Adomßent, Grahl, & Spira, 2019).

Crucial Case: Canteen

Anyone who has attended university knows that the way to students' hearts is through their stomachs. Therefore, canteen food and lunch options are an area worth mentioning in a dedicated section. Even a casual stroll through a university campus can show how willing and serious the institution is about going sustainable. While introducing recycling is a relatively easy endeavor, offering sustainable options only, i.e., removing beef or meat altogether from the menus, will result in complaints and discontent. But, it is exactly at this juncture when the university administration needs to take a stand, as at stake are credibility and integrity.

To exhibit credibility, universities might be advised to take a phased approach to sustainability. They could begin by providing sustainable catering at any university-sponsored event and/or organize a campaign to reduce food waste (Pinto et al., 2018). Next, the administration might issue guidelines for what can be ordered for small-scale events and meetings, along with a list of vetted sustainable vendors. When these practices have been in place and accepted by all parties involved, the final step of providing only sustainable menus throughout the food service system might be implemented and is more likely to be accepted, if not welcomed.

Rankings: Pros and Cons

By now, rankings as well as national and international accreditation bodies are explicitly measuring institutions' societal welfare and sustainability (Ragazzi & Ghidini, 2017). This is, of course, a positive development, as it incentivizes institutions to act accordingly in order to compete. Ecoseals of approval are even awarded, such as the EFMD's (European Foundation for Management Development) BSIS (Business School Impact System) accreditation.

However, universities need to be prudent about consistency on this matter. It will be negatively perceived if on the one hand, sustainability and societal impact appear on a university's agenda, but at the same time, it pushes in the opposite direction for the sake of rankings. What is meant by "in the opposite direction"? I'll use business schools as example. Business schools' rankings give weight to graduates' starting salaries. Therefore, schools may try to persuade students to work in the financial or consulting sector. While such work is not bad per se, students who wish to should rather be encouraged, not demotivated, to go in the direction of start-ups in the sustainability sector, where starting salaries are necessarily lower.

Universities: Speak out Loudly

Taking strong (possibly unpopular) stances on societal issues is certainly not easy. However, universities and business schools, in particular, gained a lot of visibility at the moment of the 2008 financial crisis, with fingers pointed at management schools and their curricula. Since then, universities have been expected to speak out not only on ethical leadership, but also on migration, sustainability, LGBTQ + rights, and other progressive causes.

Last but not least, an awareness of digitalization's overall societal impacts needs to be honed. As aforementioned, many will likely lose their jobs to robotics and automation, resulting in enormous challenges on a global scale. Students need to be aware of these transformations and enable to make their contributions to an equitable and sustainable world in which nobody is left behind (Kaplan, 2020b).

Presidents: Lead by Example

Finally, students will challenge not only their professors, but also their presidents, vice-chancellors, deans, and rectors. Due to their doing so, I can proudly say that my personal lifestyle has become more sustainable over recent years (with lots of room for improvement, of course), thanks to my students. In my own position, I was personally challenged on how I can support sustainability while I make myself coffee every day using a capsule coffee maker that leaves behind hundreds of nondegradable aluminum capsules each year. I have to admit that although it was staring me in the face, I didn't even notice this and was not aware of the existence of degradable or recyclable pods: just one example of students exhorting their universities to go green.

Thus, we need to constantly keep in mind that our students are watching us, and accordingly, it is incumbent upon us to listen to them (Bryman, 2008). Is there a member of the university's Board of Directors who oversees sustainability? Is sustainability part of the institution's master plan and its official mission? Are you providing a sustainability report monitoring progress and clearly stating where you want to go and what you want to achieve in the next five, 10, and 20 years? These seemingly small steps can have huge impacts.

3.5 TOWARDS A BETTER WORLD: AALTO UNIVERSITY

As case study, Aalto University showcases many of the characteristics of the university of the twenty-first century. Having only recently celebrated its first decade, interdisciplinarity is one of Aalto's cornerstones, manifested in numerous dimensions, such as how students are encouraged to approach the writing of their capstone projects and theses. Regarding responsible leadership and sustainability, this Helsinki-based higher education institution states:

> *Aalto University is a multidisciplinary community of bold thinkers, where science and art meet technology and business. We are committed to identifying and solving grand societal challenges and building an innovative future.*

As such, Aalto fosters sustainability, both in instruction and curricula as well as throughout its operations.

The Aalto Way: An Interdisciplinary, Sustainable University

Aalto is Finland's second-largest university, with nearly 20,000 students and a staff of 5,000, including nearly 400 professors. Its annual budget totals almost €400 million. Aalto was established as a merger of three higher education institutions teaching differing scientific disciplines: the Helsinki School of Economics, the Helsinki University of Technology, and the University of Art and Design Helsinki. The merger's explicit intention was to foster multi- and interdisciplinary research and teaching across the disciplines of arts, business, and technology. While interdisciplinary efforts in academia are not simple endeavors, Aalto has succeeded therein owing to broadly organized focus groups and discussions among professors and researchers coming from the various disciplines toward analyzing the challenges and opportunities of bringing various fields together (Hollmén, 2015). Aalto's slogan is "Towards a better world," and its stated mission is to shape a sustainable future. On its website, one can read:

> *Aalto's future is built upon a foundation of high-quality research, education, impact and shared values: responsibility, courage, and collaboration. We have adopted a living strategy tailored to a world in motion. Our purpose, values, and way of working define our long-term direction. We choose development areas and actions that best drive us toward our purpose. As a community, we proactively and continuously re-evaluate these choices.*

Aalto's Cornerstone: Interdisciplinarity

At its inception, Aalto was assigned a national mission to strengthen Finland's innovative capacity through art, education, and research. Multi- and interdisciplinarity are keys in positively responding to this mission, as is expressed on the university's website: "We are building a competitive edge by combining knowledge from differing disciplines and through long-term partnerships with the best universities, industry, and the business world."

The key drivers of fostering multidisciplinary education and research are Aalto's innovation and entrepreneurship "crown jewels": the Aalto Design Factory, one of three on-campus manufacturing facilities, where students can work on real-life corporate problems with companies providing financial resources; Aalto Ventures, Aalto's entrepreneurship education program; and Aalto Entrepreneurship Student Society, Europe's most active and prominent student-run entrepreneurship society. Multidisciplinarity is also the subject of a recent study by the European University Association (EUA) titled "The Role of Universities in Regional Innovation Ecosystems," which showcases Aalto as supporting entrepreneurship by ensuring a "multidisciplinary and encouraging environment, where students can meet colleagues from other disciplines through curricular or student initiatives" (Reichert, 2019).

Aalto's Thesis 2.0 Project: An Application

A very hands-on example of Aalto pursuing a multi- and interdisciplinary approach is its Master Theses program. A multidisciplinary team of two to four students is formed wherein, while each individually writes his or her thesis, they collaborate for six months on a topic assigned to them by a real business, nonprofit organization, or government agency. During this period, not only are team sessions and meetings between each student and his or her respective thesis supervisor held, but also fixed appointments with the partner organization. The "cherry on top": Each student receives a grant supporting his or her work.

The team thesis is a multidisciplinary effort, i.e., each student brings to the table his or her expertise from his or her respective academic discipline to tackle the partner organization's assigned problem. The final presentation, as well as a jointly written report, is conducted entirely in an interdisciplinary spirit, i.e., students are compelled to find a common, combined perspective to meet their assigned challenge. On Aalto's website, details are indicated:

> *The programme has been designed to facilitate students' development of "21st-century competencies," such as critical thinking and collaboration [...] A comprehensive, interdisciplinary narrative to address a complex challenge, spanning multiple disciplines, is of significantly higher value to the partner organisation than are 2-4 individual theses on narrowly defined topics. Through various approaches, methodologies, and disciplines, the goal is to deliver something greater than the sum of the theses' parts.*

Aalto's Courses: Sustainability in Education

Aalto aims to integrate sustainability into all curricula, as well as individual courses. Theretoward, Aalto is constantly revising and renewing its degree programs and course offerings. More than ten study programs entirely dedicated to sustainability figure in Aalto's educational portfolio. Examples of master's programs are "Building Technology," "Creative Sustainability," and "Environmental Engineering." Furthermore, several undergraduate degrees, courses, and electives are offered on a variety of sustainability topics across Aalto's entire course catalog. Moreover, Aalto has also produced several Massive Open Online Courses (MOOCs) on sustainability, such as "Circular.now," "Climate.now," and "Leadership for sustainable change."

Aalto's success as well as its trailblazing in the area of sustainability in education has been reported on in the *Financial Times*, whose respected business school rankings take into account best practices in sustainability, social impact, and ethics research and teaching in schools worldwide, as assessed by a panel of expert judges. Showcased in a *Financial Times* article (Jack, 2019), Aalto's sustainability efforts were described thusly:

> *All students are exposed to corporate responsibility and sustainability, with a large list of electives and specialisations. They can opt to become management professionals with a specialisation in sustainability. The creative sustainability master's programme offered jointly with the School of Arts, Design and Architecture, emphasises multi-disciplinarity, systems and "design thinking".*

The Aalto Campus: Sustainability in Operation

Not only in education and research, but also in its operations, Aalto is dedicated to sustainability. As such, its Code of Conduct defines sustainability as one of its operating principles, stating "We aim to minimize any adverse effects of our activities on the environment in all our operations."

Accordingly, Aalto constantly aims at decreasing its energy consumption and improving the energy efficiency of its physical plant. To that end, energy is largely self-produced sustainably, with the clear aim of reaching energy self-sufficiency by 2030. To achieve this objective, Aalto continuously and incrementally increases the use of solar energy and geothermal power. Since 2012, Aalto has reduced its yearly carbon dioxide emission 40%. Targets are publicly communicated, and the university is signatory to the national energy efficiency accord, part of Finland's comprehensive package of voluntary energy efficiency agreements.

4

DEGREES CONVERTING INTO LIFELONG LEARNING

Universities pride themselves, and rightly so, on being the sole issuers of recognized, accredited degrees, enabling the holder entry into the employment market. However, as aforementioned, job requirements are evolving faster than ever, which leads to a constant need for employees' upskilling and reskilling (Ates & Alsal, 2012). This, in turn, places more weight on lifelong learning, with the likely consequence of early life university degrees losing relevance (Selingo, 2017). Such a development opens the door for alternative course providers, offering new ways of certification of a learner's knowledge and skill sets, possibly depreciating traditional Bachelor's and Master's degrees' value. The job market will decide the pertinence of this evolution by hiring (or not) candidates who choose these new ways of proving their expertise.

This chapter opens with a discussion of the implications of higher education increasingly moving toward lifelong learning. One likely consequence thereof is so-called micro- and nanodegrees entering the labor market, providing universities with several opportunities, but also significant challenges. Corporate universities, particularly noteworthy and potentially threatening to higher education institutions, will be analyzed. Job markets possibly tipping the scale in their favor, supported by artificial intelligence (AI) and big data, will be addressed. As a case study, Laurie Pickard and her "no-pay" MBA curriculum-from-scratch will be presented. By successfully avoiding astronomical tuition for a degree, yet not sacrificing course quality by enrolling in Massive Open Online Courses (MOOCs) from the best universities worldwide, Pickard impressively demonstrated one way that higher education might be disrupted.

4.1 LIFELONG LEARNING PARTNERSHIPS

The importance of lifelong learning is by now acknowledged by higher education, the corporate world, governments, and society at large. Accordingly, the university of the twenty-first century has a vested interest in convincing alumni to return to their alma mater for further training and education. Moreover, ongoing collaborations with the corporate world will be crucial for a related reason; Academia most likely will need to collaborate with big tech and educational technology (EdTech) start-ups so as not to render themselves redundant. Finally, the increasing relevance of lifelong learning will most likely depreciate university degrees that workers earned in early adulthood.

Prevalent Appreciation of Lifelong Learning

The corporate world has always evolved, with industries and jobs rapidly expanding and contracting in reaction to technology and innovation, all the more so with society's digital transformation and advances in AI and robotics. The World Economic Forum recently announced an emergency for reskilling, explaining that more than a billion jobs worldwide will be transformed by technology. Chui, Manyika, and Miremadi (2016) further showed in their *McKinsey Quarterly* article that approximately 45% of labor could potentially be automated with *current technologies*. Finally, the pandemic definitely accelerated the technologization of jobs and the trend toward automation.

Because such developments will eliminate hundreds of thousands of jobs or, in the best case, transform the tasks and qualifications necessary to perform these jobs (Kaplan & Haenlein, 2020). This correctly leads to doubts as to whether one's undergraduate or even advanced degree will suffice for one's entire occupational life. Continuous learning is, therefore, in order, as employees require regular updating of knowledge and skills in order to remain relevant in their industries and workplaces. In order to respond to this new demand for lifelong learning, the current model in most higher education institutions needs to shift from focusing on preparing graduates for their first jobs toward a model wherein universities accompany them throughout their careers.

Perennial Partnering with Alumni

Higher education needs to move from mainly rendering young adults "job ready" to a lifelong companion and partnership. On the one hand, curricula for early life degrees must be designed and developed from a continuous learning perspective, and on the other, alumni need to be convinced to return to the classroom. This necessitates firstly that universities begin to be bluntly transparent with students that a Bachelor's or Master's degree will not be sufficient for succeeding in a career; rather, further learning will be needed (Dellarocas, 2018). Reading most academic programs' marketing brochures wrongly gives the impression that by completing the given course, students are set for life. Such advertising and expectation management only makes it harder to convince alumni of the opposite down the road.

Currently, many institutions encourage alumni to return for further training by giving them significant discounts and incentives. Indeed, subscription models where learners pay a regular or a one-time fee for a limited or unlimited number of courses – similar to a gym membership, but for intellectual "workouts" – might become common. Northeastern University describes such a program in its "Northeastern 2025" academic plan (Northeastern University, 2016). Such a model also better accords with the original meaning of the term "alumnus," as Chris Dellarocas (2018) pointed out:

> *The original meaning of the Latin word 'alumnus' is 'foster child'. In a world where students never really graduate, the role of the university is to take lifelong care of them, as we would take care of our true foster children.*

Permanent Cooperation with Companies

Alongside accompanying and facilitating students and alumni throughout their professional careers, higher education institutions also have an interest in building ongoing collaborations with the corporate world. Whoever has designed and executed a course or in-service training knows that the more often you teach this course for the same enterprise, the better it will be adapted to the firm's sector and specific needs. Only with time will you be able to perfect your instruction. Moreover, by cooperating with companies on a long-term basis, you also forge an ever-more-important sense of community, upon which I will expand (Komljenovic, 2019).

Moreover, cooperating with companies also helps universities to gain insight into the corporate world and its current issues and problems to ensure that the skills and competencies taught today are aligned with those needed tomorrow (Faingold, 2019). Professors who teach executives are able to take the exchanges and learnings therein back to their classrooms where they teach their younger students. This is invaluable, and accordingly, the university of the twenty-first century should enable as many of their faculty as possible to teach continuous learning modules.

Possible Collaboration with Big Tech and EdTech

Lifelong education will increasingly take place online, which demands regular updates and involves production costs that in many cases don't yet exist in universities' current budgets. It, therefore, might be beneficial or even necessary for them to partner with EdTech start-ups and big tech companies. Scott Galloway, for example, pointed out that "Ultimately, universities are going to partner with companies to help them expand. I think that partnership will look something like MIT and Google partnering" (Walsh, 2020). Although, as a counterpoint, Joshua Kim (2020) doubts the creation of these partnerships, at least on a large scale, they should not be ruled out.

The university of the twenty-first century will need to decide whether such partnerships make sense for its particular situation and context. Regardless, such collaborations will have to be carefully designed so as not to run the risk of universities being rendered obsolete. An example of such a risk is embodied in Skillshare, a New York–based EdTech start-up. Skillshare offers a subscription model for online courses: For a fee of either $15 per month or $99 a year, learners can choose from more than 20,000 courses ranging from arts, to business, to tech (Wan, 2018). To prevent such a development taking away business and revenues from traditional higher education institutions, it is crucial for universities to forge strong relationships and a sense of community with their students (see Chapter 5). Only when universities build lasting links will alumni return – either to campus or online – over the duration of their careers.

Plausible Depreciation of Early Life Degrees

The current model is to obtain the bulk of one's education in early life, which is supposed to serve for one's entire occupational life. Yet, this model no longer suffices, and as such, early life degrees have already decreased in value, or as Thomas and Brown (2011) put it, "The half-life of a skill is five years (and shrinking)." This is not to say that pursuing a Bachelor's or a Master's degree is worthless. However, the value of such degrees calculated over an entire career is depreciating. Continuous learning is the new normal, and replaces the soon-to-be outdated three-stage model of education, work, and retirement.

This devaluation of a Bachelor's degree might render it necessary to rethink several current systems, such as business models and pricing strategies. Currently, students pay a one-time fee, which usually is somehow related to both the number of credit hours and the respective degree, i.e., there is ordinarily a continuum beginning with Bachelor's, to Master's, to MBA and Executive MBA diplomas. In addition to the aforementioned subscription-based model, other arrangements might be income-sharing agreements whereby students pay the university a certain percentage of their salary for a predefined period after having earned their degree (*The Economist*, 2018). In this new era of continuous learning, higher education needs to be open to experimentation and creativity to come up with more adapted and justifiable pricing and business models (Dellarocas, 2018).

4.2 MICRO- AND NANODEGREES

The depreciation of initial three- and four-year degrees will free up resources for shorter certifications – micro- or nanodegrees – in which learners enroll throughout their entire professional career and which are particularly adapted to a model of lifelong learning. Via such shorter-duration degrees, academia will be able to rapidly respond to evolving job market requirements. Moreover, they will facilitate the introduction of a multi- and interdisciplinary approach to learning and teaching, a path that the university of the twenty-first century definitely has an interest in pursuing. A further leveraging of micro- and nanodegrees is their delivery of instantaneous gratification and qualification to learners. Yet such certification courses not only provide advantages to higher education, they also come with a set of drawbacks and limitations.

Describing Micro- and Nanodegrees

Micro- and nanodegrees can be broadly described as a course of study that is much shorter than a traditional university course and that focuses on the skills directly needed for a given job. In most cases, microdegrees cost far less than do traditional university degrees. A typical microdegree can be earned for less than €1,000 and takes a couple of weeks. Furthermore, the vast majority of such degrees are earned remotely/online, all of which render them an ideal way for working adults to continuously update their skills (Reeves, Tawfik, Msilu, & Şimşek, 2017).

Such microdegrees have their origins in the STEM (science, technology, engineering, and mathematics) disciplines, which traditionally place more value on practical skills than do other academic areas, and as such, certification of certain micro-skills is already quite common. For example, Udacity worked together with Google to develop its nanodegree as certification to become an Android Developer, Google's mobile phone operating system. This short program provides the skills that software developers require to create apps on Google's Android.

Detecting Requests and Requirements

Microdegrees have the advantage of quickly responding to the changing requirements of employers as well as student desires. A recent study by Fong, Halfond, and Schroeder (2017) showed that approximately one-third of employees born between 1981 and 1996 indicated the desire to acquire additional certifications, with many of them indicating that they do not make use of what they learned at university in their current jobs.

By offering microdegrees, higher education institutions can react faster to new demands and create content that is of direct relevance to the job market (Jackson, 2019). Anybody in academia knows that a change in curricula, even a course, can easily take one to two years, as it goes through several committees as well as accreditation bodies, whereas microcertification courses focus on emerging topics such as AI and robotics, or even more specifically on modules such as autonomous driving or the aforementioned mobile app development. In this respect, very specialized traditional degree programs might be even more at risk in the new environment of microdegrees than are more general programs providing an overview of a certain field.

Developing Multi- and Interdisciplinarity

As aforementioned, multi- and interdisciplinarity within degree programs is increasingly important. However, getting there is easier said than done, as programs are usually designed at the departmental or faculty level within a university. Whoever is already involved in creating a program bringing various disciplines together knows that while doing so is very exciting and intellectually stimulating, it also can be a serious challenge when facing such questions as whose (which department's) resources are to be used and how they will split revenues, responsibilities, and costs. Until the aforementioned necessary structural changes within faculties and universities occur, the unbundling of degrees and microcertification could be an intermediary step toward interdisciplinarity.

Another advantage of microdegrees is that they enable universities to go beyond their own walls to look for courses from other universities. This might make especial sense if a given university does not have a faculty or department in a certain discipline or subject. As a precursor thereof, one could take the example of US universities in adjoining states; For example, a Missouri resident who wishes to study art can do so at the University of Kansas and pay in-state tuition.

The same is true of a Kansas resident who wants to study mining and metallurgy in Missouri. Moreover, microdegrees could certify certain competences acquired in extracurriculars, internships, or community work. All of these competences then could be summarized in an expanded transcript appended to a traditional listing of grades and course credits, with additional certifications and badges. At Nashville-based Lipscomb University, to give another example, students can earn badges à la Foursquare (Kaplan, 2012) for a variety of skills such as presentation expertise, which are then approved and recognized by the university on an expanded transcript.

Delivering Gratification and Qualification

In addition to the aforementioned advantages of microdegrees, they can be used to provide quicker assessment of qualification within a longer degree program. This direct and nearly instantaneous assessment of learning enables students to immediately monetize the obtaining of a certain qualification and skill when searching for an internship or a full-time position, in turn facilitating and advancing competency-based education. Finally, microdegrees within a certain degree program can follow a gamification approach; When students know that they will earn microdegrees for some of the program modules, which they then can show to potential internship providers, they will likely be more motivated to go the extra mile.

Additionally, prerequisite assessment is simplified when enrolling in a microdegree module, as it can better assess a student's competencies, regardless of the source of his or her prior knowledge. In this way, issuing microdegrees helps the storytelling of the respective student, i.e., why she/he did not enroll in certain course modules, as she/he can provide proof of having mastered the material therein via a microdegree. Especially with universities increasingly enrolling those who have acquired certain competencies on the job, microdegrees might be a convenient way to facilitate this.

Discussing Drawbacks and Limitations

Micro- and nanodegrees might have their limitations and drawbacks (Ralston, 2021). Firstly, scheduling and logistics might be made difficult if students earn microdegrees from other educational institutions, or can compile an entire degree comprising multiple microdegrees. Doing so might take longer than would a traditional degree, which might not be a problem if, for example, the learner is studying part-time alongside working. Another possible drawback is that microdegrees allow for more customization of curricula, leading to higher heterogeneity among graduates' knowledge and skill sets. Currently, companies recruit from a given university and program, as they are familiar with the graduate cohort and what they have studied. A more customized approach, thus, renders detailed transcripts and expanded transcripts all the more important in order to render a student's skills and knowledge more transparent.

On a more general note, critical voices might also have an issue with such an in-demand, on-demand trajectory of a given student, arguing that there are reasons why changes in curricula and syllabi are not to be done hastily; Just because some competence might be in demand this month doesn't mean that it makes sense to integrate its acquisition into a given program. Ultimately, like all change, it will be a question of the right mix and ratio.

4.3 CORPORATE IN-HOUSE UNIVERSITIES

Corporate universities, i.e., in-house training facilities established by companies and other organizations, most likely will become more common, thereby facilitating employees' continuous upskilling and reskilling quickly responding to corporate needs, to mention just one advantage thereof. An example thereof is Google's career certificates, which in a timely move, Google established during the pandemic, impressively showing in what direction higher education might need to shift if it is to remain relevant. As corporate universities evolve and perfect the concept of continuous in-house education, they have the potential to constitute a threat to traditional universities, which will need to counter this development by pointing out corporate universities' drawbacks and limitations.

Architectures: Logic of Corporate Universities

In a way, corporate universities are a reaction to academia's flaws. Many companies started their own in-house training units as they discovered that especially business schools – but not only – did not provide students with tools to effectively tackle the real-world problems facing companies. They discovered that by creating their own trainings, they were more likely to get the managers and leaders needed to run their businesses (Nixon & Helms, 2002).

Probably, the best-known corporate universities are Hamburger University in Chicago, operated by McDonald's Corporation, or General Electric's Crotonville, established in 1956 and considered the first corporate university. While essentially a US invention, corporate universities are to be found worldwide. They are not universities in the strict sense of the word, as they usually do not grant official degrees, but rather typically limit their scope to providing job- and/or company-specific training for their own employees (Paton, Taylor, & Storey, 2004).

Benefits: Advantages of Corporate Universities

The number of corporate universities is on the rise, and according to Hoare (1999), is postsecondary education's fastest-growing sector. According to Prince and Beaver (2001), this increase is due to companies increasingly recognizing in-house universities' positive impact. Their main advantage is that they can transmit to students the skills that they will directly use in their jobs, while at the same time transmit their corporate culture and *esprit de corps*. For students, corporate universities are a good option, as they guarantee a job and a salary upon completing them. As such, corporate universities overcome two of the main critiques of traditional higher education institutions: students and their families having to repay student loans over decades and companies hiring employees not equipped with the skills they need in their jobs.

A final advantage of corporate universities is that the educators therein are often C-suite executives. Obviously, this is appealing to students, but is also a refreshing opportunity for executives and senior leaders to have direct contact with the next generation. As teachers, executives are able to directly transmit their vision as well as facilitate cultural change. Moreover, they get a sense of what young, potential employees are looking for in a good employer and help their organizations to transition accordingly.

Changes: Evolution of Corporate Universities

Corporate universities have changed over time. Nowadays, an in-house university is more than just an educational unit; It is about helping employees to achieve the objectives set by the company. In this respect, their mission has moved even closer to providing training that is directly and immediately useful on the job. However, while the first corporate universities cared only about their "graduates" being employable at their "mother" institution, nowadays they are well aware that their deliverables must help their staff remain employable elsewhere. With most of us having more than one employer throughout our professional lives, corporate universities are an important move toward employee retention, as well as an even more appealing alternative to traditional universities. Moreover, corporate universities have become more wholistic in their approaches, now playing roles in a variety of human resource aspects such as talent acquisition, onboarding, performance reviews, and employee engagement.

Furthermore – coming full circle, perhaps predictably – some corporate universities are collaborating with academia on an even higher level, i.e., obtaining international accreditation. As early as 2001, the European Foundation for Management Development (EFMD), one of the two most important business school accreditation bodies, launched Corporate Learning Improvement Process, which evaluates and accredits corporate universities in the same way as is done for business schools within the scope of its prestigious Equis label. The race is definitely on.

Drawbacks: Limitations of Corporate Universities

The obvious drawback of corporate universities is that, although some of them proudly display the aforementioned quality labels, they are not allowed to award state-accredited Bachelor's, Master's, or MBAs. However, this might not be a real limitation for long since; as aforementioned, the trend is moving away from degrees and more toward skills and competences, i.e., lifelong learning. The more companies that transition to searching for employees with the appropriate competences versus the "right" degrees, the more likely the corporate university model is to become accepted and even mainstream.

Another drawback to corporate universities is that therein, students are exposed to a single corporate culture only. Firstly, instructors at corporate universities often are not trained professors reflecting on and researching a particular subject having an overall and broad knowledge of the domain. Secondly, even if corporate universities have their employees' employability (also) beyond their own walls in mind, it is unlikely that they would discuss a competitor's success stories, although this would certainly depend upon the given instructor's approach and the organization's policy. Nonetheless, more often than not, traditional university courses are more likely to present a variety of companies and contexts in their lectures.

Example: Google, LLC

Although not a corporate university in the strict sense, it nevertheless makes sense to look at the case of Google to understand higher education's current challenges. Fortuitously, at the advent of the pandemic, Google launched its own professional trainings, imparting to participants the skills for in-demand jobs of the moment. In these Career Certificates, as Google calls its microdegrees, participants learn to become a data analyst, project manager, or UX designer. Courses are developed and taught by Google employees working directly in these areas, preparing participants with the skills they immediately need for those jobs.

Lasting just six months, Google Career Certificates cost only a fraction of the cost of a university degree. As Kent Walker (2020), Google's senior vice president of global affairs, pointed out,

> *College degrees are out of reach for many Americans, and you shouldn't need a college diploma to have economic security. [..] We need new, accessible job-training solutions – from enhanced vocational programs to online education – to help America recover and rebuild.*

In this context, Google announced the creation of 100,000 needs-based scholarships for their certificates. It furthermore announced that it will treat these certificates as equivalent to any four-year degree for related roles in their hiring policy. And if you do not wish to work for the search engine giant, Google will also help its graduates to find jobs at other companies including Bank of America, Best Buy, or Walmart (Shein, 2020).

4.4 JOBS AND JOB MARKETS

As has always been the case, it is ultimately the labor market and employers who determine the relevance of alternative certification courses offered by both academic and nonacademic players, as well as the future appeal of corporate universities, by serving as ultimate evaluators of a candidate's competence and skill set. Only if such varied paths also lead to employment will they gain in legitimacy among students and learners. The use of big data might support such a change. Udacity, a well-known MOOC platform, makes ample use of big data and serves as another example of where higher education might be headed. The university of the twenty-first century will need to think of ways to protect itself from such disruptive tendencies. An effective career service as well as the forging of strong relationships between students and their alma mater are two examples of such protective measures.

Here we'll discuss the role of job markets as ultimate accreditors of a candidate's skills and competences, as well as how big data and blockchain technology might be game changers. Udacity will be presented as potential disruptor of the sector. Finally, the importance of effective career services in universities will be underscored, as well as how, in combination with strong relationships and university community building, career services can act as strong weapons against the disruption of traditional higher education.

Job Markets as Ultimate Accreditors

Vis-a-vis corporate universities, one could state that the highest validation of a university comes from the job market itself. In the case of companies accepting microdegrees and competences and skills obtained outside the traditional higher education system, this could lead to essential problems for universities (Sindre, 2018). We already saw how Google is willing to consider their own certification courses as equivalent to four-year degrees. For the moment, however, it is still easier for companies to rely on universities to provide them with good job candidates, as it is quite difficult to figure out what a candidate is able to do by looking at a list of independent, unconnected courses and short-term modules and programs without knowing their exact content and material.

The nonprofit organization Credential Engine might be a solution to this potential threat to traditional higher education. Credential Engine's mission is to provide companies with a sort of "marketplace" that simplifies the comprehension of a given candidate's micro- and nanodegrees. Course providers register their certifications with Credential Engine, and by doing so, create standardized information about what has been learned therein, thereby facilitating the comparison and comprehension of learned content and skills.

Big Data as Powerful Indicators

Currently, employers prefer hiring preselected graduates of specific universities with particular profiles and competencies. Yet supposing an EdTech firm such as Credential Engine was likewise able to preselect candidates? Data are increasingly available at large scale, and EdTech companies have lots of it. EdTech career service platforms know which courses a student took, as well as his or her GPA and extracurriculars, thereby enabling them to potentially find the perfect student–employer match. It might only be a question of time until employers render state-accredited, official diplomas largely meaningless.

Another effective recruitment tool might be blockchain technology (Roebuck, 2019), which could record any educational activity. Due to blockchains' structures, it is impossible to change or alter any record after it has been put into the system, i.e., it is forgery proof. On blockchains, one could easily collect all courses, extracurriculars, and prior professional experience of a given candidate. Blockchains also enable companies to search for candidates with a desired profile and the exact competences and skills needed for the given position.

Udacity as Exemplary Disruptor

Nanodegree providers such as Udacity not only provide courses but also promise jobs after completion of the program. Indeed, concerning its Nanodegree Plus program costing $299 per month, Udacity even has a money-back guarantee if graduates do not find employment within six months after course completion (Metz, 2016). To be able to provide MOOC graduates with jobs, Udacity partners with companies such as AT&T, Intel, and Google, which accept Udacity courses as valid credentials for potentially hiring Udacity graduates.

According to Udacity, their microcredentials also facilitate access to education to all, regardless of one's current situation. As early as 2014, Sebastian Thrun, Udacity's founder, stated: "We are creating the nanodegree to give lifelong learners access to affordable credentials that will be recognized by employers as they move forward in their professional careers" (Falk, 2014).

Career Service as Effective Facilitator

In this new environment, universities' career services and personal development teams become all the more important. A career service division is essentially a clearinghouse serving as a bridge between the worlds of students' education and their (future) employment. For students, career service teams offer individual advice on careers and entry points, perform CV checks, and conduct interview trainings for both internships and jobs. Insights into the job world are provided via seminars, workshops, and company presentations. For companies and other employees, the university career service is the portal conduit to reaching potential employees among the student body (Cheung, 2012).

Given that external providers and EdTech start-ups are increasingly entering this universe, the university of the twenty-first century needs to provide better and higher quality career services than these new entrants do and can deliver.

Partner companies and organizations need to be extended priority access to students that goes beyond a mere presentation of their business to students. Such information sessions could also be provided by an external player. For example, a company could be directly integrated into a given course via a customized case study or with company representatives being hosted for one or more classroom sessions. Corporations could be asked to coselect students into a certain specialization or for specific modules. They can play important roles during orientation week or at graduation ceremonies, to mention just a few examples. For students, universities' career service teams will need to increasingly act as personal coaches and – in some cases – even therapists.

Relationships as Strong Protection

For the time being, university degrees are still the standard entry to a good-paying job, and micro-degrees are considered an add-on to traditional education, not a substitute therefor. Employers who have not yet partnered with MOOC providers such as the aforementioned Udacity are still reluctant to consider such courses to be real qualifications for hiring purposes. But, as we evolve to lifelong learning, the question is how long universities can maintain the status quo.

In the battle of being cannibalized by nanodegrees, universities have a strong weapon: strong relationships with students as well as companies, which we will discuss in detail in the next chapter. It was recently discussed that career services of traditional universities need to outperform those of EdTech start-ups, corporate universities, and MOOC providers, and provide companies with the better graduates and graduates with better jobs. This is possible through customized and personalized guidance, interview preparations, and personal development. Several further possibilities for fostering strong, long-lasting such relationships are the topic of Chapter 5.

4.5 MBAS AND THE NO-PAY MBA

It's no secret that that tuition for MBAs has skyrocketed over the last decades. Laurie Pickard, therefore, decided to go a different route and fashioned her own MBA curriculum combining several MOOCs from prestigious institutions worldwide, costing her only a fraction of what a traditional MBA would. Her line of thinking and approach to this possibly first-of-a-kind endeavor serves as case study. The established MBA market will be reviewed and contrasted to Pickard's self-styled "No-Pay MBA." Pickard's success on the job market illustrates the potential relevance of such alternative, nonofficial, nonaccredited degrees. The fact that an individual can pull this off shows that it is not necessary to be an online giant such as Google or LinkedIn to challenge the current model, and gives a detailed illustration of higher education's upcoming transformative journey.

Laurie Pickard's Self-made MBA Degree

Laurie Pickard graduated in 2003 from Oberlin College, where she earned a Bachelor's in politic science. From 2006 to 2008, she pursued graduate studies at Temple University, where she earned a Master's in geography and urban studies. Thereafter, she joined the Peace Corps in Nicaragua, where she stayed for over four years, taking on various roles in various organizations. It was there that she began considering an MBA, as she felt that she needed an education in business and management to advance professionally.

While initially considering various programs in the United States and Europe, one of Pickard's friends took a finance MOOC on the Coursera platform. This gave Laurie the idea of putting together her own, customized MBA curriculum by combining several MOOCs from prestigious universities such as Harvard, Wharton, and Yale. No sooner said than done, Pickard began her customized program in August 2013 and finished it in May 2016 with far more course credits than that of any traditional MBA curriculum provides or requires. Given that Pickard's spouse, a diplomat, was stationed in Rwanda, the online aspect of this self-made MBA was an additional advantage. Regarding cost, Pickard spent less than $1,000 for her entire program.

The Traditional MBA Market

The first MBA was awarded in 1908 by Harvard Business School. It combined courses in quantitative subjects, such as accounting and finance, with courses in soft skills, including entrepreneurship and leadership. Not much has changed since. Either one or two years in length, MBAs are structured around core courses in the first part and electives and specialization options thereafter. In addition, participants usually pursue an internship during the pursuit of a degree and work on a thesis or capstone project in the MBA's final phase. Generally speaking, an MBA is intended to provide enrollees, who often already have several years of professional experience, with a general overview of management disciplines toward their next career steps.

Much has been said and written about MBAs, even including their having been proclaimed dead. This is certainly due to their moving toward shorter, more continuous learning modules, but also, and even more so due to the nearly prohibitive tuition. At the best US business schools, such as Stanford Graduate School of Management, tuition has reached more than $200k. In particular in the wake of the 2008 financial crisis, MBAs have been sharply criticized for failing to educate their bearers on ethics, which is likely another reason for declining enrollment, even at the most prestigious schools such as Sloan, Kellogg, or Wharton.

The No-Pay MBA

To develop her MBA curriculum, Laurie Pickard reviewed the MOOCs offered by top business schools across the world. In all, she completed 27 online courses, far more than any traditional MBA offers. Modules ranged from Corporate Finance taught by Aswath Damodaran at Stern School of Business to Marketing taught by David Bell, Peter Fader, and Barbara Kahn at Wharton; to a course titled "How to Finance and Grow Your Startup – Without VC" taught by John Mullins at the London School of Business. These are all not only prestigious business schools, but also names of world-class academics, which one rarely gets at such a density in a traditional MBA earned at a single institution.

Obviously, Pickard's MBA had a couple of drawbacks, such as the missing classroom interaction. Also, the networking aspect with classmates was missing, which is the main argument for many MBA enrollees to earn a traditional degree and take on the aforementioned high tuition. However, Pickard was not in it for the network, but rather for the development of her skills. Further insights into her MBA journey are available at www.NoPayMBA.com. This blog, which Pickard began during her studies, had two purposes: firstly, to help others interested in the same adventure; and secondly, as a public commitment to help her through this journey, which necessarily requires high self-control and strong motivation.

The Job Market and Coursolve

The biggest drawback and unknown element of such a self-constructed MBA was certainly the question of how the job market would value a nonofficial program and degree. However, already during her studies, Pickard again found a solution – again online – to this challenge. Via the help of Coursolve, a start-up connecting MOOC enrollees with actual company projects, Pickard found her internship. As the final project for her Foundations of Business Strategy course, taught by Michael Lenox of UVA's Darden School of Business, Laurie worked for Coursolve, remotely conducting a strategic analysis for them, once again not necessitating her relocating from Rwanda.

Although Coursolve, created by Nabeel Gillani while he earned a Master's degree in learning and technology at the University of Oxford, no longer exists, the idea of linking MOOC students with organizations and companies worldwide has been picked up by others. One of Coursolve's key partners was Michael Lenox in the context of his MOOC, where he invited any type of organization to solicit course participants to help them with actual business problems. More than 100 organizations responded and could count on the work and effort of on average four students per project.

Laurie Pickard's Post-MBA Career

Laurie Pickard's post-MBA career is as impressive as her original endeavor. Firstly, Pickard continued her blog and wrote a book titled *Don't Pay For Your MBA* (Pickard, 2017), which describes in detail how one should proceed in developing one's personalized education in business and management. While her compilation of MOOCs was not accredited as an official degree, Pickard earned much recognition therefor from the media. *Fortune* magazine, for example, declared Pickard "a household name in the world of MOOCs." Moreover, her journey was covered by *Bloomberg Business*, the *Financial Times*, *Time* magazine, and *The Wall Street Journal*, to mention just a few publications.

In August 2017, Pickard joined Class Central, a review site for MOOCs, as partnership lead and MOOC report editor. For two years, she worked for this start-up, remaining in the field of online education. Since August 2019, Laurie is PIVOT manager at Resonance, a consulting firm specializing in the design of action-based strategies, the development of strategic partnerships, and other intersector collaborations, specifically in frontier markets. She then moved back to the United States, where she resides in Washington, DC.

5

BUILDINGS, BONDS, AND BABIES: WE ARE FAMILY

Universities are about more than teaching material or awarding diplomas, fortunately; they're about having memorable experiences, creating networks for life, sometimes even finding one's significant other. University is about relationships and belonging to a community consisting of alumni, students, professors, staff, and beyond. While academic content can, to a certain degree, be commodified (Naidoo, 2003) and early-life degrees might lose their value, relationships are much harder to replace. However, higher education institutions do not always behave like they're in the relationship business, thereby rendering them vulnerable to disruption. Community is, therefore, the subject of this chapter.

Herein, we'll look at several examples of what universities can do so that students have a peak experience, ranging from student societies to the canteen's food selections. The next section "turns around" alumni and how they can be significantly beneficial to a university in a variety of ways if, and only if, they forged a strong attachment to their alma mater during their studies. The remaining stakeholders of a university, i.e., professors, administrative staff, external partners, and the general public, will also be addressed. Real estate and physical plant will be discussed as a further path to strong community building, while offering a broader outlook on the usefulness and importance of buildings for the university of the twenty-first century. Finally, my own alma mater as well as employer, ESCP Business School, the European School of Commerce Paris, will be presented as a case study.

5.1 STUDENTS: TIME OF MY LIFE

Like Jennifer Grey and Patrick Swayze having their final dance to "Time of My Life" in the classic *Dirty Dancing*, students need to "get the same feeling" during their studies. The university of the twenty-first century must adopt a student-centric approach (Pucciarelli & Kaplan, 2016) without demanding astronomical tuition fees, which in itself is decidedly not student-centric. Higher education needs to provide full service and support to students, treating them as customers in nonacademic areas and as stakeholders with regard to academic matters. Extracurriculars such as sports and student societies are already known to increase student satisfaction rates. Field trips create valuable experiences for future alumni, which they remember for a lifetime. Again, hearkening back to sustainability, a university's meal options and cafeteria are crucial to student satisfaction. Finally, students take notice when administration makes gestures acknowledging their importance to the institution.

Service and Support

Benjamin Franklin said "It takes many good deeds to build a good reputation, and only one bad one to lose it." So it is with universities vis-à-vis students: Students might enjoy the best courses, have a great time, and then one (unnecessary) bureaucratic SNAFU, can destroy the established goodwill. Students should be considered customers facing the university administration. Yet, this approach must be limited to the nonacademic aspects of higher education, such as a school's visa department. The customer relationship should not be applied to academics, as altering them as per client-centric considerations would be detrimental to a university's reputation (Nixon, Scullion, & Hearn, 2018). In academics, students are stakeholders, not customers: Their opinions on academic matters should be taken into account, but faculty has or should have the final say.

Take Oxford University, where the student services team is explicitly tasked with delivering a "magical, memorable, and meaningful Oxford experience" (Brooking, 2020). A former student described the team's service orientation as similar to that which you would expect on an upscale cruise ship. To realize this aim, service teams need to be trained and encouraged to find solutions instead of adhering to outdated regulations. To ensure that they are able to respond to students' requests, such teams must be sufficiently staffed. If budgets do not allow for additional hiring, processes need to be revised, simplified, and made transparent in such a way that existing teams are able to provide service instead of bureaucracy.

Sports and Student Societies

"Something for everyone" describes student societies well. At the University of Nottingham, for example, one can join the Extreme Ironing Society, where excitement is injected into this ordinarily tedious household chore. Or, if you're a

Nicholas Cage fan, you can join his appreciation society at the University of Sussex, where students watch his films together. Student societies and sports are an important part of university life. Many students would likely state that the work they do and what they learn in such societies is at least as important as their coursework. Societies foster opportunities to make friends, network, and find personal fulfilment (Archbold & O'Hagan, 2011).

Alongside the fun, participation in student societies also helps to reduce dropout rates and increase students' postgraduation employment chances (Gallagher & Gilmore, 2013). Having taken part in student societies can make the difference on a student's CV when applying for internships and jobs, rendering his or her profile just a little bit more interesting than that of a nonparticipating applicant. In societies, students learn in-demand skills such as teamwork, leadership, problem-solving, and time management. Moreover, participation in societies enables students to be exposed to disciplines distant from their area of academic study, thereby fostering multi- and interdisciplinarity. Often societies even work for the university: organizing events, helping to recruit and welcome new students, or during integration weeks. Given all this, the university of the twenty-first century should heavily support student societies and help them in their development, even if some of them tend to lean more toward the purely fun.

Souvenirs and Study Trips

"Anyone who goes travelling has stories to tell." This is the opening line of Matthias Claudius' poem "Urians Reise um die Welt" (*Urian's Voyage Round the World*) written in 1785, and now a well-known German proverb. Field trips are often mentioned by students and alumni as one of the most memorable experiences of their time at university, which is not surprising, as they constitute a break in the study routine. Field trips are clearly not only educational but also create many possibilities for having fun and getting to know fellow students on another level. In this respect, incorporating such trips into a program's early stages might be even more useful.

Budgetary considerations notwithstanding, such trips should definitely be part of the curricula, as the memories that they create vitally attach their participants to their alma mater, which is of essence in the longer term (Andre, Williams, Schwartz, & Bullard, 2017). Additionally, such trips are also a good way to market a program to prospective applicants. Finally, one does not have to travel to the other side of the world to have an exciting trip: A neighboring country or even domestic travel can certainly be a success. This should be the preferred option in any case for sustainability reasons, as it enables traveling overland, as opposed to by air.

Snacks and Satisfaction

Once again, the way to students' hearts is through their stomachs. A recent Technomic (2019) study showed that only 33% of US students are satisfied with eating options at their universities. Thus many of them eat off campus, which might divert them from developing an attachment to their alma mater. In order to know what students want in terms of food service, regular surveys should be conducted, while not sacrificing sustainability.

Food plays an even more important role in executive education. As such, the *Financial Times* (FT) included it as a specific criterion in its annual business school rankings. One of this ranking's top slots is recurrently occupied by Stanford

University's Graduate School of Business, whose chef, Raul Lacara, has cooked for the likes of the Dalai Lama and former US Secretary of State Condoleezza Rice. Together with his team, Lacara has scrutinized executives' food allergies and dietary preferences, and prepares meals accordingly. A dietician ensures that food options are nutritious and healthful. Moreover, special requests are also catered to, for example providing a special cheese that one executive ate in his childhood; or ordering special water for another executive who was reluctant to drink California tap water. This might seem excessive, but given the tuition that enrollees pay, it might be a good relationship building strategy.

Sympathy and Senior Management

Leading by example, the senior management team of the university of the twenty-first century must show interest in the students (Mina Montez, Wolverton, & Gmelch, 2002). This must go beyond the university president giving welcome speeches during induction week or at graduation ceremonies. As we all know, it's often the little things that can make a big difference. For example, a university president could occasionally congratulate a student for having organized a successful event under the auspices of a student society. While this will not always be feasible, students are keenly aware of such gestures, as reports thereof make their way around the student body, generating goodwill.

An official form thereof has been established at Wharton Business School, which introduced the position of Dean of Happiness. In an attempt to ease student stress and increase student satisfaction, Wharton created this position, whose role it is to keep students cheerful and content. To achieve this objective, the Dean of Happiness provides students with his or her mobile number in case they need to contact her quickly and directly. Experience shows that students are well aware of the value of the dean's time, and do not abuse this calling option. Moreover, student satisfaction clearly increased, as shown in survey results. Furthermore, it seems that the creation of the Happiness Dean also led to more alumni donations: our next topic.

5.2 ALUMNI: MEMORIES AND MOMENTS

"Memories and moments," as sung by country recording artists Tim O'Brien and Darrell Scott, are key to alumni's attachment to their alma mater. Alumni are a strong, if not the strongest asset, that universities have, as graduates remain alumni throughout their lives, as opposed to faculty and staff, who might move on to other job opportunities. Attached alumni can serve as ambassadors proudly promoting their alma mater. They moreover can (and should) return to the lecture hall for lifelong learning and executive education. Finally, alumni are potential donors, having become an increasing source of a university's finances. Usually alumni are connected via a university's alumni association which, alongside higher education in general, has undergone significant transformations (Gallo, 2012).

Alumni as Assets

Alumni are certainly strong assets to any higher education institution. In order to create good relationships with them, it is crucial to treat them as such from the outset, i.e., as soon as they step onto campus for the first time, or put another way: Students become alumni. And if students were not convinced of the university's interest in them during their studies, it will be hard to persuade them to become involved alumni thereafter. Additionally, the necessary relationship building and bonding is much easier done with students, who are in daily contact with the university, than as alumni, where the touchpoints are fewer and less regular (Sung & Yang, 2009).

Usually alumni are organized in alumni associations, which are independent of their respective universities, rendering it important to maintain good relationships therewith. Alumni associations serve as bridges between the university and its alumni, so that the more integrated and informed an association is about what is going on at their institution, the better. Accordingly, alumni associations must have a seat at the table of important decisions. Finally, remember that not all alumni are members of an alumni association, as the latter are often still run on the basis of annual membership dues. Nonetheless, nonmember alumni are valuable assets for a university as well; at least they can be, if there is infrastructure in place to enable getting in touch with them.

Alumni as Boosters

Alumni can be your best ambassadors, boosting your marketing campaigns and messages for free to coworkers, family members, friends, and anybody else who's interested (or not); so it's no surprise that referrals from alumni or students count for over half of incoming students in many programs. While in marketing terms, one refers to such players as advocates (Weerts, Cabrera, & Sanford, 2009), in order to become a brand's advocate, clients need to be very satisfied with the product. With education, the path to winning over alumni is actually shorter, as they are part of the product, i.e., they advertise themselves. Accordingly, they cannot entirely have been dissatisfied with the product, which could turn the potential for positive word of mouth on its head.

It needs to be clear, though, that for alumni to boost a university's communications, marketing, and recruiting, they need to be aware of the message to transmit. While obviously, alumni who are successful in their careers already promote the educations that they received, if you want them to diffuse precise messages, you need to tell them directly what these are. As a marketer, I can say that the most efficient way to get a message across is to follow the KISS principle, i.e., keep it short and simple.

Alumni as Clients

Referring to alumni as clients certainly shocks less than describing students as clients. Yet as aforementioned, alumni can come back to their university as enrollees for executive education, where the term "client" is more appropriate than it is for early-life degree programs. Moreover, as alumni can become donors, they should consider it advantageous to be viewed as clients. However, alumni should not be treated as ordinary clients, but rather as preferred clients. This status might, for example, confer discounts on continuous learning programs or dedicated, alumni-only training.

Finally, regarding alumni-as-clients, instead of a transactional model, a *relational model* should be used. Accordingly, functional customer relationship management (CRM), as we call it in marketing jargon, is of the essence (Payne & Frow, 2005). Collecting and handling data of individual alumnus-clients enables universities to not only sell them continuing education but also consult with them to deliver customized career and personal development guidance. And as any marketer having researched CRM would tell you, customer retention is far easier and beneficial than new customer acquisition, and almost nowhere is this truer than in the higher education sector.

Alumni as Benefactors

Alumni may act as benefactors and donors of sometimes astronomical sums (McAlexander, Koenig, & Schouten, 2006). As an example, I'll cite Kenneth Griffin, a successful manager in the financial sector, who has donated a total of $150 million to his alma mater, Harvard University (Herbst-Bayliss, 2014). However, universities need to tread carefully so as not to reduce alumni to mere ATMs: Alumni will donate *if they feel that it is not only money that you want from them.* Moreover, and justifiably, they want something in return for their support, be it simple acknowledgment, contact with students, or a say in what happens to their donations. A good way to frame it is to imagine how good a friend you'd need to become to someone in order to ask them for money. Almost on the familial level, isn't it?

Yet alumni must be considered more than simply potential benefactors. Before becoming donors, alumni are our students, enrollees in executive education, mentors, speakers whose voices are heard, or conduits for communicating messages. Only if they have played those roles during their studies will they be willing to participate in their alma mater's funding. Ignoring this incurs a high price, as not only is the university of the twenty-first century increasingly dependent upon such funding, but also, and not to be underestimated, it will need the help of alumni to promote programs, recruit, provide collaborations for research, and many more areas of development.

Alumni and Associations

Alumni associations are critical to every university of the twenty-first century. Accordingly, as does their alma mater itself, alumni associations need to undergo transformations in order not to be disrupted by new players in academia. One of those players, LinkedIn, has become fierce competition to alumni associations. In particular, those who built their mission around providing alumni with contacts to other alumni for career networking, have slowly but surely been replaced by LinkedIn, where it is far easier to find alumni whose CVs are more up-to-date than they are in a database on the alumni association's website.

Thus alumni associations need to find other ways to appeal to their members. Unique or exclusive job opportunities are one possibility. Indeed, it is not rare that committed and successful alumni first seek job candidates from their alma mater before considering other applicants. Another way is to foster interest by informing alumni of what's going on at their alma mater. Finally, many associations have moved from the annual dues model toward a lifetime membership model (often equal to five or ten years of annual fees combined) instead of having to renew membership annually.

5.3 STAKEHOLDERS: ONE BIG (HAPPY) FAMILY

While students as well as alumni are important university stakeholders, there are more groups to be considered in the university community if it is to form one big, happy family (as sung with gusto by the entire cast of Disney's *My Friends Tigger & Pooh*): Here we speak of faculty, traditionally considered the most important stakeholders. Administrative staff, corporate and institutional partners, as well as a university's local and regional environment, comprise the remaining stakeholder cohort. All of these belong to a university's community, and all must find their place in the university of the twenty-first century (Marshall, 2018). The art of community – and every university president's challenge – is to balance differing needs and desires, often contradictory, of these various groups.

Professors

Faculty members are usually uninterested in administrative matters, with the exception of those among us who aspire to deanships, rectorates, and presidencies. However, they will involve themselves therein if they believe that things are not working as they should. This is completely understandable, as most professors remain at their respective institutions until they retire. As such, among all of the various stakeholders, professors have the strongest interest in their university running well. Students are only there for a matter of years, alumni are far away, and administrative staff often also moves on after a few years at an institution.

The issue is that in the past, regarding many administrative matters, faculty had decision-making powers. While this worked when competition was less fierce and funding more secure, the university of the twenty-first century will need more experienced administrators and experts in various fields, such as student recruitment. Faculty members therefore feel their authority decreasing, and will demand detailed explanations why decisions have been made one way or another. After all, it's a good sign when faculty members are interested in what happens at their institution, as the opposite would be detrimental. Therefore, even if difficult or contentious issues arise, it is worth the administration's welcoming faculty input. After all, without faculty, there is no university. And without motivated faculty, there is no sustainable university.

Professional Service Staff

Universities often forgot and still forget the importance of support staff in giving more weight to faculty's opinions and desires. Of course this is justified when it comes to academic affairs. However, in other matters, the university of the twenty-first century has a strong interest in closely listening to its administrative staff, who most likely have vast expertise in admissions, marketing, and career guidance, just to name a few areas.

If not managed carefully, this partial transfer of power from faculty to administrative staff leads to tension and dissatisfaction. Nonetheless, the importance of professional service staff is undisputed. Scott Galloway, for example, boldly points out in a widely read and searing article, that:

> *The most value-added part of a university is not the professors; it's the admissions department. They have done a fantastic job creating the most thorough and arduous job-interview process in modern history, between the testing, the anxiety, the review of your life up until that point, the references you need.*
>
> (Walsh, 2020)

Partners

Corporate and institutional partners are another stakeholder group to address. The European Commission (2013), for example, recommends that universities strengthen relationships with the corporate world as a way of increasing higher education's access to resources, to design and offer joint programs, or to work on common research questions, co-obtaining new insights and knowledge. Chaired professorships financed by a company are one way of incorporating the corporate world into a university. Another example is corporate scholarships, which also nurture links between a university and a company.

To facilitate and nourish such partnerships, the university's corporate relations department will be a key player not only in connecting professors with companies, but also in managing student–company relationships. Often companies enter into a partnership with higher education institutions in order to obtain privileged access to students and potentially hire them. This mechanism needs to be carefully orchestrated, as students don't necessarily want to work for their university's partner firms; and by the same token, students' "dream companies" might not be interested in a partnership with a given university.

Public

The university of the twenty-first century also needs to consider the broader public, especially within its local and regional environment, as a key stakeholder group. It clearly is to a university's benefit to foster good relationships with local and regional authorities, and even more so with its direct neighborhood (Lising, Astin, & Cress, 2000). To foster this linkage, university administration should participate in and support events in the surrounding community, and vice versa: Members of the community should be regularly invited to university events. This will help to forge reciprocity, which is of immense value in creating win-win opportunities between universities and their immediate surroundings (Altbach, Berdahl, & Gumport, 1999).

The pandemic has put such benefits on display, so to speak, in a variety of dimensions. Confronted with social distancing measures, universities have found themselves facing serious space scarcity, often not able to host the entire student population. We know of several cases of local governments and NGOs jumping in to providing their available rooms and buildings for instructional purposes. Waterhouse (2000) gave further examples such as Derby University, where a dedicated organization and infrastructure for meeting long-term needs of the local community has been established. In addition, on an ongoing and regular basis, Derby offers a variety of courses (e.g., in computer literacy) to locals.

Parity

The university of the twenty-first century needs a strong community and functional community-building measures in order to flourish in the ever-more-competitive higher education market. Every stakeholder group, including students, alumni, faculty, auxiliary staff, institutional and corporate partners, and the broader public, plays a vital role in the university community. To feel appreciated, these stakeholders must be given the sense that their voices count; and that no one stakeholder group is considered more important than another, which, when not handled delicately, creates headaches for the university. As aforementioned, faculty for one, is used to prevailing in disputes, which might not be feasible in the future, at least not to the extent enjoyed up until now.

The evolution toward parity among stakeholders results in complicated tradeoffs and questions: Should an alumnus who desires to teach at his or her alma mater be allowed to do so? Should s/he get hiring priority? Supposing s/he is hired, and turns out not to be a good pedagogue? While in the past, the alumnus probably would politely have been asked to look for other options such as joining a university's career service team to share his or her expertise, future universities might go in a different direction, e.g., offering coaching to improve his or her teaching skills. Another dilemma: Should students be permitted to schedule an event on campus or an excursion that conflicts with the course schedule? While in the past, the answer would simply have been "no," courses can be rescheduled and timetables adapted. While academics must remain the priority for any higher education institution, the university of the twenty-first century might need to show flexibility in handling such dilemmas (Kaplan, 2018a).

5.4 THE PHYSICAL PLANT: LET'S HANG ON

Buildings are a vital element to fostering strong community spirit. It would be wrongheaded to believe that owing to digitalization, physical buildings are becoming obsolete. The financial temptation for a university's administration to adopt such a line of thinking might be huge, but would be a mistake. With courses increasingly moving online, buildings might even be more important than before. So as Barry Manilow sings, let's hang on…to our buildings. In this new context, students will need to be attracted to campus, as the need to attend live courses decreases. Work spaces such as anti-cafés, for example, will become essential to fostering exchange among students, continuing education enrollees, alumni, and professors, thereby strengthening the aforementioned vital attachment of these stakeholders to their institution. Furthermore, physical buildings are necessary for innovative teaching, fostering multi- and interdisciplinarity, as well as serving as a communications and marketing vector.

Buildings Build Strong Communities

Community building is of utmost importance at the university of the twenty-first century, as by now everybody should understand, and buildings are needed to realize this goal (Temple, 2008). Yet instead of huge amphitheaters, higher education institutions should dedicate an increasing portion of their space to teamwork and collaboration, as well as encounters and exchanges between fellow students, between students and faculty…and why not alumni and the entire university community?

Space designs in the form of the anti-café will become standard to enable such vital community building. Anti-cafés could be described as modern versions of coffeehouses, whose main purpose is not to encourage consumption, but rather to provide a workspace with the option of coffee or a snack. The French business school EM Lyon has an anti-café on campus where students, alumni, and school partners work in a collaborative environment that resembles more an airport lounge than a traditional café. To involve a university's entire community, furthermore, libraries, cafeterias, quads, or event spaces can be opened to the broader public, which might furthermore open up new revenue streams.

Buildings Strengthen Vital Attachment

More particularly, buildings must strengthen vital attachment of students to their university (Muhammad, Sapri, & Sipan, 2014). They accordingly need to enable a stimulating student life, host student societies and sports clubs, and foster a welcoming atmosphere. Only thusly will students (and professors for that matter) want to come to campus and in turn become strongly attached to their alma mater. Remember:

With more and more courses being taught online, there is less and less direct reason to be on site. Students attending classes from home might become attached to their living rooms rather than to their institution (Rovai & Wighting, 2005). Therefore, students will need to *want* to come and spend time on campus, necessitating the university's providing appealing, high-quality spaces featuring inviting interior designs.

Yet, there is even a further reason why buildings are needed. Online teaching and learning, though often cited as democratizing education, can also potentially increase social disparities. During the pandemic, it was brought home to us that not all students had laptops at their disposal, an issue that could still be fixed by providing them with the necessary IT. However, it also became evident that not everybody has spacious living quarters, much less students, who overwhelmingly live in shared housing, making it difficult for them to focus on online classes. Thus remote learning might actually thwart fostering a diverse student body, an issue demanding every university's attention (cf. chapter 3).

Buildings Enable Innovative Teaching

As aforementioned, the future of learning and teaching is about finding the right mix of online and on-site instruction. In general, offline pedagogy becomes more interactive in nature with an increasing variety of teaching and learning formats. Accordingly, classrooms and auditoriums need to be easily adjustable with respect to their layout: They need to be easily expandable, contractible, and alterable according to the instructional method used. Technology-enabled active learning (TEAL) demonstrates how such an evolution can be supported by physical spaces. The TEAL classroom at Yale University, for example, has room for more than 100 students sitting at 10 to 15 tables, each equipped with a flat screen, in addition to five large projection screens distributed around the room. This setting allows the instructor to switch between short lecture modules and hands-on group work, where the just-learned material can immediately be discussed.

Moreover, universities are increasingly providing space for start-up incubators and accelerators, helping to inculcate an innovative, entrepreneurial spirit. These incubators often require a lot of physical space, and are designed to enable students and alumni to work on their innovations, ideas, business models, and implementation. They also provide space where partnerships between the university and corporate partners can be fostered and developed.

Buildings Foster Multidisciplinary Research

Alongside teaching, research can be facilitated via the setup of buildings and room structures. The necessity for conducting research multi- and interdisciplinarily was previously made clear. Accordingly, closed offices and a lack of space to meet up and exchange with one's peers will not foster collaboration between colleagues, let alone across disciplines and faculties.

More and more higher education institutions are establishing interdisciplinary research buildings, one of the most recent being University of Texas, which built a 150,000-square-foot (about 14,000 sq. meters) facility at cost of $100 million. The building's architecture is designed to enable researchers from various departments and faculties to share workspaces as well as laboratories. Instead of permanently assigning a space to one or several faculty members, room is allocated on a short-to-longer-term basis upon request, thereby accommodating the specific needs of a given research team. To ensure that projects are mainly interdisciplinary in nature, a review team consisting of faculty members – another way of restoring faculty input – evaluates proposals toward the allocation of space (Martinez, 2020).

Buildings Market the Institution

A final way of making good use of physical buildings is their capacity as marketing collateral. There are reasons why prospective students take campus tours: They want to feel the school's atmosphere and "vibe." Buildings market a place and help to attract the best students, professors, and support staff. Take Clemson University's Watt Family Innovation Center, which showcases the South Carolina institution as being highly attuned to new technologies. Watt features approximately 200 touch screens that students activate by swiping their student cards; a 10-meter high interactive video wall at the structure's center; and additional space where faculty can test out the latest educational technologies and tools (Scar, 2016).

Some universities go even further in using buildings' marketing potential. The Ecole Polytechnique Fédérale de Lausanne, a Swiss university specializing in natural sciences and engineering, opted for its conference, library, and study center to resemble an oversized Swiss cheese, with floors that rise up internal hills and dip down into valleys, so that even the space yodels. And recalling walking the walk with respect to sustainability and real estate, buildings are a further marketing vector for the university of the twenty-first century.

5.5 ESCP: IT ALL STARTS HERE

It All Starts Here is not only a song by the US band Magic Man, but also my own alma mater's current slogan. ESCP indeed invented the concept of the business school more than two centuries ago, hence it is where it all began. To survive two world wars, not to mention other cataclysmic events, a strong community was essential. The choice of a business school as our last case study makes sense (in addition to the fact that it is my own institution), as ESCP is often cited as having an especially strong sense of community. Moreover, the fact that ESCP is located in six cities across Europe, leading to a highly international alumni network dispersed worldwide, renders its community building of particular interest (Kaplan, 2018b). Two ESCP areas are particularly noteworthy: its career service, dedicated to students and companies alike; as well as an ambitious construction project, pushing ESCP even closer to becoming a university of the twenty-first century.

ESCP: The World's First Business School (Est. 1819)

ESCP, the European School of Commerce Paris, had its origins in Paris in 1819, as its name indicates. It was established by a group of businessmen and scholars, including the economist Jean-Baptiste Say and noted merchant Vital Roux. ESCP's establishment marks the beginning of business school history. While this was clearly not the inception of the concept of business administration and management, it represents a landmark in management education and a more institutionalized and structured approach thereto.

In 1973, ESCP was again a pioneer, establishing the first cross-border, multicampus business school, enabling its students to move across and study in various countries over the course of their studies. In 2019, ESCP, now established in Berlin, London, Madrid, Paris, Turin, and Warsaw, celebrated its 200th birthday, poised to (re)invent the business school once again. In addition to its own campuses in six major European metropoli, ESCP also has partnerships with more than 100 universities and schools worldwide in a variety of disciplines within and beyond business and management. As of now, ESCP's annual budget totals approximately €120 million, mostly coming from tuition – at least for the moment.

A Cross-border, Cross-campus Student Community

With campuses in six countries, ESCP's more than 7,000-strong enrollment in 30 undergraduate, graduate, and post-graduate degree programs is highly diverse. Over the academic year, the school organizes events aimed at community building and bringing together key stakeholders. One of these events, organized by a team of students with only a little assistance from the institution, is the ESCP Regatta.

The regatta encompasses what ESCP is all about. Once a year, students from all six campuses, as well as members of staff, faculty, and alumni, come together for a weekend on [the island of] Ischia off of Italy's western coast. The regatta is a unique opportunity to fully exploit the potential of a multicampus school and to broaden and strengthen the esprit de corps that is key to the ESCP community and for which it is known. Celebrating its 10th anniversary in 2017, the ESCP Regatta has become a highlight of the school's sports, networking, and social calendar.

A Worldwide Alumni Community

The ESCP Alumni Association was established in 1872, some 50 years after the school's founding. Its mission is to bring together the community of approximately 65,000 alumni across the globe, promoting solidarity among them and providing them with a collection of services and tools. The association helps ESCP graduates in their first steps in their professional lives and offers individual coaching to alumni further on in their careers. Its network includes about 150 professional, geographic, corporate, and social interest groups, supported by more than 700 alumni delegates and experts, who collaborate to organize about 500 events annually.

ESCP's alumni association recently faced two challenges. First, having originated as a French business school, the association has increasingly taken steps to internationalize its activities and services. Mainly based in Paris, the association now has staff in London and Berlin. Yet what might seem like a no-brainer created some unforeseeable issues. For example, the idea of publishing the monthly alumni magazine fully in English was opposed by several veteran alumni, who wanted the magazine published in French only. Secondly, as is the case with many alumni associations, membership has decreased over time. To counter this development, the association decided to move from an annual dues model to one of lifelong membership, as described previously.

A Career Service Dedicated to Both Students and Employers

To link the student community with corporate partners, ESCP has dedicated career service teams across its six campuses. These career service and company relations services act as an interface, particularly concerning internships. Whenever students graduate, the alumni association takes over this task.

Recruiting Days are one example of the alumni association's activities. During these multiday events, students from the various campuses convene on one of ESCP's campuses along with companies trying to attract the best talent. However, Recruiting Days go beyond a mere career fair: Companies are extended the opportunity to organize hiring interviews with potential candidates, and many students thus have jobs lined up even before their graduation. Moreover, career service teams also organize large-scale events that go beyond matching job recruiters and finding internships: The annual Conference on Sustainable Innovation in Berlin is such an example. During this two-day happening, the first day is dedicated to high-profile speakers from businesses, political institutions, and civil society, aimed at inspiring students to become ethical and accountable managers. During the second day, several workshops structured along the 17 sustainable development goals (SDGs) are conducted, where students work in small teams together with experts on specific challenges that these experts currently face in their organizations.

An Ambitious Real Estate Project Leading ESCP into the Future

Finally, ESCP's ambitious real estate project will be presented. While there are plans to invest in the physical plants of all of ESCP's campuses, with a global budget of more than €100 million, the specific plans for ESCP Berlin will be described. After Paris, ESCP Berlin's campus is the largest in terms of student and faculty, enrolling more than 1,000 students per year. More than tripling its population in less than four years, the campus's usable area became constrained. This led to the renovation of an additional 3,000 square meters of an annex located in one part of our current venues that until recently was completely gutted and vacant.

This new space provides additional classrooms, offices, and a large amphitheater, in addition to a cafeteria, a cutting-edge library, and a learning center. Moreover, a significant part of the additional space is specifically dedicated to increasing ESCP's entrepreneurship activities. The initial ideas theretoward surrounded helping start-ups planning to enter the German market (and vice versa), in particular focusing on start-ups with a multinational founder team, consistent with ESCP's DNA; and the establishment of a networking club that brings together founders, academics, students, and of course the alumni community.

6

UNIVERSITIES: BETTER SAFE THAN SORRY

Herein, we have seen how higher education is undergoing several transformations, one or more of which potentially lead to its disruption. The Covid-19 pandemic accelerated and underscored the sector's digitalization, with online courses and even online degrees increasingly visible on the educational landscape. Artificial intelligence (AI) advances will permanently change both teaching and learning. We saw that society's digital transformation should also impact the content taught at universities, demanding a stronger focus on the development of skills such as adaptability and autonomous learning versus pure knowledge acquisition. The university of the twenty-first century should teach multi- and interdisciplinarily, as well as educate responsible and sustainability-minded leaders, all while walking the talk themselves. We discussed traditional, state-accredited degrees being threatened by micro-degrees, corporate universities, and the job market itself, with companies gradually placing less weight on such classic, early-life degrees, and education evolving toward lifelong learning and continuous re- and upskilling. Finally, the role of communities and relationships was addressed, showing their vital importance to a university's ability to avoid its potential disruption. In this last chapter, I briefly summarize and further highlight some of the aforementioned threats to universities, which should, inter alia, be understood as a call for action for the university of the twenty-first century to fight to stay relevant, and not succumb to its progressive, steady dismantling (Kaplan, 2020c).

6.1 UNIVERSITIES DELIVER HIGH-CLASS PEDAGOGY, YET…

Universities still have preeminence as education experts, and threatening them on this front will be quite challenging. Yet, higher education institutions will avoid disruption only if they remain at the top of the teaching game and start to make deliberate use of the tools available to them in the digital sphere (and beyond) to improve their pedagogy and remain at the forefront. Applying learning analytics and AI to move toward adaptive learning and a customized teaching approach is just one example of how universities will need to change their habits and ways of doing things. Those who do not will likely be left behind.

Moreover, over the past few decades, higher education has increasingly placed more weight on research versus teaching regarding professors' assessments and career trajectories. We already saw that moving toward multi- and interdisciplinarity will necessitate a change in mindset. Research output is – at least presently – more objectively measurable than is teaching performance, which is often assessed by student evaluations only, which are not always objective. This possibly leads academia to prioritize research over teaching quality. Moreover, research directly boosts a university's reputation and its rankings, whereas pedagogy, thus far, plays a less direct role therein.

As discussed, the sector's digital transformation in general and in pedagogy in particular could be a game changer. In theory, it is possible to analyze the relationship between successfully completing a course and the improvement of certain skills. As such, a given course's quality and effectiveness could be measured objectively, likely shifting weight back from research to teaching. Such a shift could better showcase a university's teaching expertise. As a consequence and also for reputational reasons, universities might need to refocus on their pedagogical core. As such, applying the right digital tools and technologies to free up time for professors' research might enable the university of the twenty-first century to invest enough time in pedagogy to stay on top of its game in this vital area.

6.2 UNIVERSITIES PROVIDE OFFICIAL DEGREES, YET...

Universities often feel safely ensconced, and do not view big tech or edtech as serious challengers of their turf, as they currently are both the quasi-exclusive issuers of degrees and the brandishers of prestigious labels from various national as well as international accreditation bodies. Yet accreditation bodies, too, are increasingly searching for new markets and additional funding. Moreover, degrees are now issued by nonuniversity institutions, too. Code University, for example, obtained the right to issue state-accredited degrees by Germany only a couple of years after its opening. Moreover, we extensively discussed the fact that the official, early-life degree might be slowly replaced by continuing education and other forms of (nonofficial) degrees and certifications.

In this context, we also discussed the fact that the highest validation of a university comes from the job market itself. Currently, employers still prefer to hire preselected students from specific universities, who possess a certain profile and set of competencies. Universities historically have helped students in their internship or job searches via the institution's career services. Recently, however, universities have begun to outsource this value proposition to edtech start-ups, which offer career guidance to students, mostly free. Based on their profiles, students are matched with potential employers based on what the latter are looking for. As these platforms bring together several universities and employers, as opposed to individual higher education institutions, networking effects of significant scope exist. Couple the capability of nonuniversity players identifying and proposing the perfect employer–employee match with companies moving away from basing their recruiting on traditional degrees to lifelong learning and shorter but regular course work, and we see some threat on the horizon.

Another issue arises with respect to the aforementioned importance of community and student attachment. Graduates are quite appreciative of having obtained the job of their dreams through their alma mater's help. If in the future, students instead attribute this achievement to an edtech platform, to whom will they owe their gratitude? Grateful alumni are more likely to donate their money as well as their time to their alma mater. It might therefore not be wise for the latter to outsource such high-value services. At the very least, it is incumbent upon universities to come up with ways for their career service to complement that outsourced to edtech platforms.

6.3 UNIVERSITIES FOSTER STRONG NETWORKS, YET...

In the previous paragraph, I cited the importance of communities and networks built in and around a university. As aforementioned, students' best memories of their time at university most likely include having created relevant networks, making friends, and, in some cases, finding a life partner. Students' attachment to their university is accordingly highly influenced by such strong, positive memories.

However, going on three decades now, the Internet has also served as a networking platform or marketplace for finding social contacts beyond the university walls. Any alumni association is in denial if it doesn't consider LinkedIn its competition. Moreover, Instagram, Tinder, and Facebook often help us meet friends and significant others; and more recently, edtech start-ups have virtually breached the ivory tower.

Although finding friends can be facilitated digitally, it still is easier to find them "live." As aforementioned, strong relationships between a university and its various stakeholders is certainly one of the most effective weapons against disruptive developments. As most friendships are forged outside the lecture hall, going for coffee or beers, universities have a vested interest in organizing networking and other events that students will remember long after graduation. Moreover, alumni associations need to find new and innovative ways to create added value over LinkedIn and other social media platforms. Several examples of how they could achieve this aim have been given.

6.4 UNIVERSITIES COMBINE ALL OF THE ABOVE, YET...

A final argument often made for universities' belief that they are disruption-proof is that they represent hubs combining all of the above: teaching expertise, community and networking, certification, prestige, and reputation. Without a doubt, universities do have these, as they constitute microenvironments of opportunities, experiences, and memories. However, this is only true if universities actively work on and constantly improve on each of these dimensions.

Universities cannot leave whether the individual components of their raison d'être function or not up to chance. Just witnessing people meeting in classrooms and in hallways will not be enough; the university of the twenty-first century needs to proactively organize networking events and engineer occasions for social encounters. It has already been shown in several industries that digital transformation and disruption do not occur all at once, but rather proceed progressively. Once again, the music industry can serve as an example of a sector that was disrupted gradually: Napster served as content provider, while MySpace provided a platform for fans getting closer to their beloved recording artists. Crowdfunding sites such as Kickstarter partly replace a record label's artists and repertoire (A&R) division.

To avoid its likewise disruption, the university of the twenty-first century must consider and intensively work on all aspects outlined above. In addition, a further avenue to avoiding their potential dismantling is to strengthen their value proposition and the corresponding communication thereof. Often, not even a university's senior administration is capable of clearly articulating its institution's current value proposition. Such an environment facilitates start-ups' journey to disruption of higher education one irreversible step at a time.

6.5 UNIVERSITIES, BE AWARE OF THE "YETS": IT'S TIME TO ACT!

I began by saying that universities have been generally resistant to change. Looking back over the past few centuries, it is true that higher education's conservatism is both frightening and frustrating. It is also true that until now, their business-as-usual strategy has served them well. However, recent evolutions in the market show that this time, it really might be wiser to consider some important transformations. The sector's digitalization alone – propelled, accelerated, and accentuated by the pandemic – should already be the push for universities around the world to reflect on what to do differently and what new paths and directions they should take in order to better be safe than sorry (Kaplan, 2020c). University of the twenty-first century, it's time to act!

BIBLIOGRAPHY

Adomßent, M., Grahl, A., & Spira, F. (2019). Putting sustainable campuses into force: Empowering students, staff and academics by the self-efficacy green office model. *International Journal of Sustainability in Higher Education, 20*(3), 470–481.

Alsadoon, E. (2020). The impact of an adaptive e-course on students' achievements based on the students' prior knowledge. *Education and Information Technologies, 25*(5), 3541–3551.

Altbach, P. G., Berdahl, R. O., & Gumport, P. J. (Eds.). (1999). *American higher education in the twenty-first century: Social, political and economic challenges*. Baltimore, MD; London: The Johns Hopkins University Press.

Altbach, P. G., Reisberg, L., & Rumbley, L. E. (2009). Trends in global higher education: Tracking an academic revolution, report prepared for the UNESCO 2009 world conference on higher education. UNESCO. Retrieved from https://unesdoc.unesco.org/ark:/48223/pf0000183168

Andre, E. K., Williams, N., Schwartz, F., & Bullard, C. (2017). Benefits of campus outdoor recreation programs: A review of the literature. *Journal of Outdoor Recreation, Education, and Leadership, 9*(1), 15–25.

Archbold, J., & O'Hagan, J. (2011). *Student societies & clubs: Current structures and historical context, with special emphasis on arts/cultural societies*. Dublin, Ireland: Trinity Long Room Hub.

Ates, H., & Alsal, K. (2012). The importance of lifelong learning has been increasing. *Procedia – Social and Behavioral Sciences*, *46*, 4092–4096.

Baer, L. L., & Carmean, C. (2019). *An analytics handbook - moving from evidence to impact*. Ann Arbor, MI: Society for College and University Planning.

Bertrand, W. E. (2010). Higher education and technology transfer: The effects of "Techno-Sclerosis" on development. *Journal of International Affairs*, *64*(1), 101–119.

Bloch, J. (2008). Plagiarism across cultures: Is there a difference? In C. Eisner & M. Vicinus (Eds.), *Originality, imitation, and plagiarism: Teaching writing in the digital age*. Ann Arbor, MI: University of Michigan Press.

Boden, D., & Borrego, M. (2011). Academic departments and related organizational barriers to interdisciplinary research. *Higher Education in Review*, *8*, 41–64.

Bowen, W. G. (2013). *Higher education in the digital age*. Princeton, NJ: Princeton University Press.

Brooking, P. (2020). *Learn just what it takes to deliver a five-star service*. Oxford, UK: The Oxford Said Review, Oxford University.

Brown, M., McCormack, M., Reeves, J., Brooks, C., & Grajek, S. (2020). *Educause 2020 horizon report – Teaching and learning edition*. Boulder, CO: Educause.

Bryman, A. (2008). Effective leadership in higher education: A literature review. *Studies in Higher Education*, *32*(6), 693–710.

Callahan, D. (1980). Goals in the teaching of ethics. In D. Callahan & S. Bok (Eds.), *Ethics teaching in higher education, the hastings center series in ethics* (pp. 62–80). New York, NY: Springer.

Carbonell, J. R. (1970). AI in CAI: An artificial intelligence approach to computer aided instruction. *IEEE Transactions on Man-Machine Systems*, *11*(4), 190–202.

Carter, D. (2011). Ga. Tech to host disabled STEM students in Second Life. *eSchool News*, March 2.

Cheung, R. (2012). Advancing career centers in higher education: Contextual and strategic considerations. *Asian Journal of Counselling*, *19*(1&2), 115–125.

Chui, M., Manyika, J., & Miremadi, M. (2016). Where machines could replace humans—and where they can't (yet). *McKinsey Quarterly*, July 8.

Council of the European Union. (2014). Conclusions on efficient and innovative education and training to invest in skills – supporting the 2014 European semester, February 24. Retrieved from http://www.consilium.europa.eu/uedocs/cms_Data/docs/pressdata/en/educ/141138.pdf

Davis, J. R. (1997). *Interdisciplinary courses and team teaching*. Phoenix, AZ: American Council on Education/Oryx Press Series on Higher Education.

Dellarocas, C. (2018). Higher education in a world where students never graduate. *InsideHigherEd.com*, August 1.

European Commission. (2013). Communication from the commission to the European Parliament, the council, the European economic and social committee and the committee of the regions, European higher education in the world, Brussels, July 11. Retrieved from http://ec.europa.eu/transparency/regdoc/rep/1/2013/EN/1-2013-499-EN-F1-1.Pdf

Faingold, A. M. (2019). *Association between recruiters' perceptions of education delivery mode and applicants' workplace readiness*. Walden Dissertations and Doctoral Studies. Minneapolis, MN: Walden University.

Falk, T. (2014). How a MOOC could get you a job, Udacity introduces the "nanodegree.". *ZDNet*, June 16.

Fong, J., Halfond, J., & Schroeder, R. (2017). *The changing landscape for professional and continuing education in the US*. Washington, DC: Center for Research and Strategy, UPCEA.

Friga, P. N., Bettis, R. A., & Sullivan, R. S. (2003). Changes in graduate management education and new business school strategies for the 21st century. *Academy of Management Learning and Education*, 2(3), 233–249.

Gallagher, D., & Gilmore, A. (2013). Social integration and the role of student societies in higher education: An exploratory study in the UK. *International Journal of Nonprofit and Voluntary Sector Marketing*, *18*(4), 275–286.

Gallo, M. (2012). Beyond philanthropy: Recognising the value of alumni to benefit higher education institutions. *Tertiary Education and Management*, *18*, 41–55.

Gibbons, M., Limoges, C., Nowotny, H., Schwartzman, S., Scott, P., & Trow, M. (1994). *The new production of knowledge. The dynamics of science and research in contemporary societies*. London, UK: SAGE Publications.

Gibbs, P., & Murphy, P. (2009). Implementation of ethical higher education marketing. *Tertiary Education and Management*, *15*(4), 341–354.

Goodman, J., Melkers, J., & Pallais, A. (2019). Can online delivery increase access to education? *Journal of Labor Economics*, *37*(1), 1–34.

Hao, K. (2019). China has started a grand experiment in AI education. It could reshape how the world learns. *MIT Technology Review*, August 2.

Haring-Smith, T. (2012). Broadening our definition of diversity. *Liberal Education*, *98*(2), 6–13.

Herbst-Bayliss, S. (2014). Hedge fund manager Griffin gives $150 million to Harvard. *Reuters*, February 20.

Hoare, S. (1999, November). Have a nice MBA. *Human Resources*, pp. 74–79.

Hollmén, S. (2015). *The pedagogical challenge of interdisciplinary university programs*. synnyt/origin | special issue. Helsinki, Finland: Higher Arts Education.

Holmberg, B. (2005). *The evolution, principles and practices of distance education* (p. 11). Oldenburg, Germany: Studien und Berichte der Arbeitsstelle Fernstudienforschung der Carl von Ossietzky Universität Oldenburg [ASF].

Huang, M.-H., & Rust, R. T. (2018). Artificial intelligence in service. *Journal of Service Research*, *21*(2), 155–172.

Jack, A. (2019). Social purpose: How business schools around the world measure up - best practice examples of sustainability, ethics and social purpose. *Financial Times*, October 21.

Jackson, N. C. (2019). Managing for competency with innovation change in higher education: Examining the pitfalls and pivots of digital transformation. *Business Horizons*, *62*(6), 761–772.

Jarvis, C. L. (2020). The flip side of flipped classrooms. *Chemical and Engineering News*, *98*(3).

de Jong, S. P. L., Smit, J., & van Drooge, L. (2016). Scientists' response to societal impact policies: A policy paradox. *Science and Public Policy*, *43*(1), 102–114.

Kaplan, A. (2012). If you love something, let it go mobile: Mobile marketing and mobile social media 4×4. *Business Horizons*, *55*(2), 129–139.

Kaplan, A. (2014a). European management and European business schools: Insights from the history of business schools. *European Management Journal*, *32*(4), 529–534.

Kaplan, A. (2014b). Old wine in new bottles? *Hindustan Times*, October 22.

Kaplan, A. (2018a). "A school is a building that has 4 walls - with tomorrow inside": Toward the reinvention of the business school. *Business Horizons*, *61*(4), 599–608.

Kaplan, A. (2018b). Towards a theory of European business culture: The case of management education at the ESCP Europe business school. In G. Suder, M. Riviere, & J. Lindeque (Eds.), *The Routledge companion to European business* (pp. 113–124). London, UK: Routledge.

Kaplan, A. (2020a). Covid-19: A (potential) chance for the digitalization of higher education. In P. Bunkanwanicha, R. Coeurderoy, & S. Ben Slimane (Eds.), *Managing a post-covid19 era, ESCP impact papers* (pp. 307–311). Paris, France: ESCP Business School.

Kaplan, A. (2020b). Sustainability: Students spur universities. *Sustpost*. Retrieved from https://www.sustpost.com/2020/06/28/sustainability-students-spur-universities/

Kaplan, A. (2020c). Universities, Be aware: Start-ups strip away your glory. *EFMD Global Blog*, May 11.

Kaplan, A., & Haenlein, M. (2009a). Consumer use and business potential of virtual worlds: The case of Second Life. *International Journal on Media Management*, *11*(3/4), 93–101.

Kaplan, A., & Haenlein, M. (2009b). The fairyland of Second Life About virtual social worlds and how to use them. *Business Horizons*, *52*(6), 563–572.

Kaplan, A., & Haenlein, M. (2010). Users of the world, unite! the challenges and opportunities of social media. *Business Horizons*, *53*(1), 59–68.

Kaplan, A., & Haenlein, M. (2012). The Britney Spears universe: Social media and viral marketing at its best. *Business Horizons*, *55*(1), 27–31.

Kaplan, A., & Haenlein, M. (2016). Higher education and the digital revolution: About MOOCs, SPOCs, social media and the cookie monster. *Business Horizons*, *59*(4), 441–450.

Kaplan, A., & Haenlein, M. (2019). Siri, Siri in my hand, who is the fairest in the land? On the interpretations, illustrations and implications of artificial intelligence. *Business Horizons*, *62*(1), 15–25.

Kaplan, A., & Haenlein, M. (2020). Rulers of the world, unite! the challenges and opportunities of artificial intelligence. *Business Horizons*, *63*(1), 37–50.

Kaplan, A., & Pucciarelli, F. (2016). Contemporary challenges in higher education – Three E's for Education: Enhance, Embrace, Expand, IAU HORIZONS. *International Universities Bureau of the United Nations*, *21*(4), 25–26.

Keating, J., & Nourbakhsh, I. (2018). Teaching artificial intelligence and humanity. *Communications of the ACM*, *61*(2), 29–32.

Kent, W. (2020). A digital jobs program to help America's economic recovery. *Google.org*, July 13.

Kim, J. (2020). Why Scott Galloway is wrong about higher ed's big tech future. *InsideHigherEd.com*, July 1.

Komljenovic, J. (2019). Making higher education markets: Trust-building strategies of private companies to enter the public sector. *Higher Education*, *78*, 51–66.

Leckart, S. (2012). The Stanford education experiment could change higher learning forever. *The Wired*, 28 March.

Lising, A. A., Astin, H. S., & Cress, C. M. (2000). Community service in higher education: A look at the nation's faculty. *The Review of Higher Education*, *23*(4), 373–397.

Lynch, M. (2019). Machine intelligence, schools in China, and you. *The Tech Edvocate*, April 5.

Marshall, S. J. (2018). Internal and external stakeholders in higher education. In S. J. Marshall (Ed.), *Shaping the University of the future* (pp. 77–102). Singapore: Springer.

Martinez, J. (2020). New building aims to promote interdisciplinary research. *UTEP Magazine*, January 22.

McAlexander, J. H., Koenig, H. F., & Schouten, J. W. (2006). Building relationships of brand community in higher education: A strategic framework for university advancement. *International Journal of Educational Advancement*, 6, 107–118.

Metz, C. (2016). Code school Udacity promises refunds if you don't get a job. *Wired*, January 13.

Mina Montez, J., Wolverton, M., & Gmelch, W. H. (2002). The roles and challenges of deans. *The Review of Higher Education*, *26*(2), 241–266.

Mucharraz, Y., & Venuti, F. (2020). Online learning can still be social, 10 keys to building a supportive digital community of learners. *Harvard Business Publishing Education.* Retrieved from https://hbsp.harvard.edu/inspiring-minds/online-learning-can-still-be-social

Muhammad, S., Sapri, M., & Sipan, I. (2014). Academic buildings and their influence on students' wellbeing in higher education institutions. *Social Indicators Research*, *115*, 1159–1178.

Naidoo, R. (2003). Repositioning higher education as a global commodity: Opportunities and challenges for future sociology of education work. *British Journal of Sociology of Education*, *24*(2), 249–259.

Nedbalová, E., Greenacre, L., & Schulz, J. (2014). UK higher education viewed through the marketization and marketing lenses. *Journal of Marketing for Higher Education*, *24*(2), 178–195.

Nixon, J. C., & Helms, M. M. (2002). Corporate universities vs higher education institutions. *Industrial and Commercial Training*, *34*(4), 144–150.

Nixon, E., Scullion, R., & Hearn, R. (2018). Her majesty the student: Marketised higher education and the narcissistic (dis) satisfactions of the student-consumer. *Studies in Higher Education*, *43*(6), 927–943.

Northeastern University. (2016). *Academic plan: Northeastern 2025*. Northeastern University. Retrieved from https://www.northeastern.edu/academic-plan/plan/. Accessed on August 26.

Obama, B. (2015). Speech at Georgia tech, March 15. Retrieved from https://obamawhitehouse.archives.gov/the-press-office/2015/03/10/remarks-president-announcing-student-aid-bill-rights

Pappano, L. (2012). The year of the MOOC. *New York Times*, November 2.

Paton, R., Taylor, S., & Storey, J. (2004). Corporate universities and leadership development. In S. John (Ed.), *Current issues in leadership development* (pp. 103–124). London, UK: Routledge.

Payne, A., & Frow, P. (2005). A strategic framework for customer relationship management. *Journal of marketing*, *69*(4), 167–176.

Pickard, L. (2017). *Don't pay for your MBA: The faster, cheaper, better way to get the business education you need.* New York, NY: Amacom.

Pinto, R. S., dos Santos Pinto, R. M., Melo, F. F. S., Campos, S. S., & Cordovil, C. M. D. S. (2018). A simple awareness campaign to promote food waste reduction in a university canteen. *Waste Management*, *76*, 28–38.

Prince, C., & Beaver, G. (2001). The rise and rise of the corporate university: The emerging corporate learning agenda. *International Journal of Management in Education*, *1*(2), 17–26.

Pucciarelli, F., & Kaplan, A. (2016). Competition and strategy in higher education: Managing complexity and uncertainty. *Business Horizons*, *59*(3), 311–320.

Ragazzi, M., & Ghidini, F. (2017). Environmental sustainability of universities: Critical analysis of a green ranking. *Energy Procedia*, *119*, 111–120.

Ralston, S. J. (2021). Higher education's microcredentialing craze: A Postdigital-Deweyan critique. *Postdigital Science and Education*, *3*(1), 83–101.

Reeves, T. D., Tawfik, A. A., Msilu, F., & Şimşek, I. (2017). What's in it for me? Incentives, learning, and completion in massive open online courses. *Journal of Research on Technology in Education*, *49*(3–4), 245–259.

Reichert, S. (2019). *The role of universities in regional innovation ecosystems*. Brussels: European University Association.

Roberts, H., Cowls, J., Morley, J., Taddeo, M., Wang, V., & Floridi, L. (2020). The Chinese approach to artificial intelligence: An analysis of policy, ethics, and regulation. *AI & Society*. Retrieved from https://link.springer.com/article/10.1007/s00146-020-00992-2

Robinson, K. (2011). *Out of our minds – learning to be creative*. Oxford, UK: Capstone.

Roebuck, K. (2019). 5 ways blockchain is revolutionizing higher education. *Forbes*, January 2.

Rovai, A. P., & Wighting, M. J. (2005). Feelings of alienation and community among higher education students in a virtual classroom. *The Internet and Higher Education*, *8*(2), 97–110.

Rubio, D., Lastra, C., Frey, C. B., Colclough, C., Jonsson, O., de Tena, C. L., & Menéndez, I. (2019). *European tech insights 2020*. Madrid, Spain: IE University.

Scar, K. (2016). Clemson – Clemson University has officially opened the doors of the new watt family innovation center. *newsstand.clemson.edu*, January 19.

Selingo, J. J. (2017). The future of the degree: How colleges can survive the new credential economy. *The Chronicle of Higher Education*.

Shein, E. (2020). Google's new certificates help people get jobs in analytics, UX, project management without degrees. *TechRepublic*, September 4.

Sindre, G. (2018). Lean and agile higher education: Death to grades, courses, and degree programs? In D. Parsons & K. MacCallum (Eds.), *Agile and lean concepts for teaching and learning* (pp. 155–169). Singapore: Springer.

Snow, C. P. (1963). *The two cultures: and a second look*. Cambridge, UK: Cambridge University Press.

Sobczak, A., & Mukhi, U. (2016). He role of UN principles for responsible management education in stimulating organizational learning for global responsibility within business schools: An interview with Jonas Haertle. *Journal of Management Inquiry*, *25*(4), 431–437.

Straumsheim, C. (2015). Ed tech's funding frenzy. *Inside Higher Ed*, July 24.

Sung, M., & Yang, S.-Un (2009). Student–university relationships and reputation: A study of the links between key factors fostering students' supportive behavioral intentions towards their university. *Higher Education*, *57*, 787–811.

Technomic. (2019). *2019 college & university consumer trend report*. Technomic. Retrieved from https://www.technomic.com/reports/consumer/consumer-trend-reports/college-and-university

Temple, P. (2008). Learning spaces in higher education: An under-researched topic. *London Review of Education*, 6(3), 229–241.

The Economist. (2018). Income-share agreements are a novel way to pay tuition fees. *The Economist*, July 19.

Thibierge, C. (2020). CovidCampus. *Blogthib*. Retrieved from https://www.blogthib.com/?s=covidcampus

Thomas, D., & Brown, S. J. (2011). *New culture of learning: Cultivating the imagination for a world of constant change*. North Charleston, SC: CreateSpace Independent Publishing Platform.

Tienda, M. (2013). Diversity ≠ inclusion: Promoting integration in higher education. *Educational Researcher*, 42(9), 467–475.

Todd, L. (2017). A professor built an AI teaching assistant for his courses - and it could shape the future of education. *Business Insider*, March 22.

Walsh, J. D. (2020). The coming disruption - Scott Galloway predicts a handful of elite cyborg universities will soon monopolize higher education. *New York Intelligencer*, May 11.

Wan, T. (2018). Can a subscription model work for online learners and teachers? Skillshare just raised $28 million to find out. *Edsurge*, July 23.

Waterhouse, R. (2000). The distributed University. In P. Scott (Ed.), *Higher education reformed* (pp. 45–58). London and New York, NY: Falmer Press.

Weerts, D. J., Cabrera, A. F., & Sanford, T. (2010). Beyond giving: Political advocacy and volunteer behaviors of public university alumni. *Research in Higher Education*, *51*, 346–365.

Williamson, B., Eynon, R., & Potter, J. (2020). Pandemic politics, pedagogies and practices: Digital technologies and distance education during the coronavirus emergency. *Learning, Media and Technology*, *45*(2), 107–114.

Zawacki-Richter, O., Marín, V. I., Bond, M., & Gouverneur, F. (2019). Systematic review of research on artificial intelligence applications in higher education – where are the educators? *International Journal of Educational Technology in Higher Education*, *16*, 39.

INTERVIEWS (SELECTED)

GRZEGORZ MAZUREK, RECTOR KOZMINSKI UNIVERSITY, POLAND

(1) **How will higher education's digitalization transform teaching and learning?**

In terms of teaching the following trends can be observed:

- the emergence of new educational content providers (MOOCs), independent from universities and the educational system (national, European, etc.), offering various formats of educational services (courses, training, quasi-diploma programs);
- the emergence of new educational formats of universities; for them, it is mostly an opportunity to enter new markets with educational services and branding (e.g., for top world universities it will be the entry with online certification programs into emerging markets);
- the modification of classic educational services (Bachelor or Master or MBA programs) through a blended-learning formula to make the transfer of knowledge, skills, and competences more attractive. The aim of such activities is also cost-effectiveness and the acquisition of new groups of students (less classes on-campus -> decrease in the costs of studying).

In terms of learning, the digitalization contributes to broadening access to knowledge and changing the formulas of knowledge transfer. Students have the opportunity to benefit from more and more educational products/"studies" offered by an increasing number of potential providers, not only universities.

Digitalization also contributes to the increasing range of possible ways of taking advantage of education – smartphonization makes it possible to study "on the way," while doing something else (driving, exercising, etc.).

(2) **What academic contents and skills should universities teach?**
Universities are spaces for development, not just for acquiring specific competences for career building. This mechanistic perspective of the university (career, profession, competences necessary for work) is a threat to the idea of the university. The university should train students to be value contributors in the future world. Therefore, apart from hard competences connected with a given professional development, students should shape and develop such qualities as: curiosity, critical thinking, entrepreneurial drive, leadership, caring for others. It is particularly important that, in the technological world, students of each field of study, especially those from the STEM area, should have their "hard" curriculum blended with content coming from humanistic disciplines (philosophy etc.).

(3) **How will degrees and certification look like in the future?**
In my opinion, the standard model: bachelor, master, PhD/MBA will gradually be broken. Both students and employers will accept other ways of confirming knowledge, competences, and skills. It will be a wide set of certificates, master classes, development programs, annual or semi-annual programs, even

computer games results. Surely the providers of such certificates will be (and are) not only the universities. The key issue for the acceptance of such development will be the recognition of these alternative systems and certification bodies throughout the education system (ministries, universities, accreditation bodies). The sooner the system acceptance of such alternative solutions takes place, the sooner the education landscape will change.

(4) **Who is and what role, according to you, does a university's community play in the future?**
This is a serious challenge because universities are losing their monopoly on knowledge creation. Research is more and more often created by companies/corporations for whom it has a strictly utilitarian value – research is for the commercial good, and thus, by implication, for society. Scientific research, especially in the area of management, is not promoted strongly enough among the representatives of the business world, which results in its hermetic character – society (and business) in such a case ceases to trust business schools, which requires undertaking an in-depth discussion on the relevance of research in the discipline of management sciences and the usefulness of its results for society.

Universities are certainly a forge of staff for business and institutions, they should be like a hub – where different thoughts, approaches, and people meet, creating value for society in a networked way.

(5) **Will the change in higher education be transformative or disruptive, and why? In case of disruption, what could and should universities do to counter their potential disruption?**
These two changes are happening simultaneously; alternative education providers are developing rapidly, but COVID-19 also forced all schools to make internal, evolutionary but nevertheless valuable changes. I don't think that universities have to look at

MOOCs as competitors – a university can offer much more value than online education offered by platforms. I also think that the demand for education will grow rapidly due to social and economic changes (the post-COVID crisis, digital transformation) and the Life Long Learning trend will continue.

(6) **In summary, how would you describe the university of the twenty-first century?**
University of twenty-first century? it is a space for development, closely connected with many other key players in the social and economic landscape; developing young personalities who understand the VUCA world, who are socially responsible; university of the future is creating important social attitudes, creating research needed by society (and business), relevant to problems and issues of importance to societies. University must be an authority for societies in the twenty-first century, as so many other institutions lose it in these difficult times.

JEAN-LUC NEYRAUT, DEPUTY DIRECTOR GENERAL IN CHARGE OF EDUCATION, RESEARCH AND TRAINING PARIS REGION CHAMBER OF COMMERCE AND INDUSTRY, FRANCE

(1) **How will higher education's digitalization transform teaching and learning?**
In a digital world, teaching face-to-face is becoming rare and its relative cost high. Face-to-face training phases will only be attractive if they provide great added value. Why travel, which is expensive in terms of time and expense, if you can benefit from the same online learning?

The challenge for training institutions will be to value their contribution as a unique contribution to learning; they will find there the sources of differentiation to strengthen their competitiveness. More than content, the way of learning will be even more decisive tomorrow than today.

(2) **What academic contents and skills should universities teach?**
More than content, it is the way of transmitting it that will be important in the digital world of tomorrow.

Universities need to cultivate their identity based on their capacity to produce knowledge. Learning to learn is essential in tomorrow's fashion. Training through research is an undeniable asset for fostering creative and innovation capacities, needed by businesses and modern societies more broadly, regardless of the sector of activity.

The soft skills that we talk about a lot today and which should not be neglected can be acquired in the context of educational situations created for learning.

(3) **How will degrees and certification look like in the future?**
A distinction should be made between initial training diplomas and executive education programs. The initial training programs will provide basic knowledge, general culture, and ability to lifelong learning. The value of diplomas may continue to be attested by accreditation bodies. The most prestigious will be promoted by strong, world-famous brands (Harvard, La Sorbonne, HEC Paris, London School of Economics).

As concerned executive education, the position of universities will be challenged by programs giving rise to capitalizable units, assessed by professionals. What better certification of an acquired skill than that shared by an experienced professional? In this game, LinkedIn is better positioned than universities.

(4) **Who is and what role, according to you, does a university's community play in the future?**
First of all, let us note that the university community must first and foremost extend beyond the members of its faculty. Like business schools, the university community

of tomorrow includes all stakeholders: professors, educational supervisors, students, alumni, partner companies, local authorities. All must contribute to making the student experience a unique and irreplaceable experience. More than today, transversal work between all stakeholders will generate value for student training.

(5) **Will the change in higher education be transformative or disruptive, and why? In case of disruption, what could and should universities do to counter their potential disruption?**

The disruption will come from the entry of new players into the higher education sector. Several factors favor this trend. Education is an attractive market. A recent study published by McKinsey shows that over the past 15 years spending on education has increased by more than 50%, while the price of discretionary goods and services has fallen by 30%.

In addition, the individualization of training paths enabled by digitization leads to a new way of consuming education. A multiplicity of offers in multiple formats is the new competition that higher education institutions will have to face.

To resist these disruptive offers, universities will have to refocus on their two main distinctive skills: knowledge production and educational engineering.

(6) **In summary, how would you describe the university of the twenty-first century?**

The twenty-first-century university is a great place to come to learn skills that cannot be found elsewhere. One can take part in top-notch research seminars and master classes where innovative ideas and concepts are discussed. The available equipment contributes to the uniqueness of the face-to-face experience; technical platforms mobilizing the best virtual reality solutions and significant computing capacities allow knowledge to be understood and immediately put into practice.

But the university is above all a place of meeting and confrontation with other students and with professional circles. The labs allow students to test their ideas and easily create their own start-up. As a place open to the world, the university welcomes all types of profiles, from inexperienced students to employees who supplement their skills or pursue retraining. Everything is set up so that the student experience is organized as a continuum between online work and face-to-face studies.

The university has become one of the hearts of the city, which comes alive day and night, embodied in a physical place, but mostly accessible digitally to support the development of skills for all citizens.

WIM DE VILLIERS, RECTOR AND VICE-CHANCELLOR STELLENBOSCH UNIVERSITY, SOUTH AFRICA

(1) **How will higher education's digitalization transform teaching and learning?**
Lockdown restrictions on physical contact and large gatherings forced universities to temporarily suspend face-to-face tuition and switch to emergency remote teaching, learning, and assessment. And while there have been some challenges, the transition to the new teaching mode has generally been so successful that it is bound to have a lasting effect on what we offer to whom, and how. The greater use of information and communications technology (ICT) in learning and teaching is set to both broaden and deepen education, not only through fully online learning but also blended and hybrid modes, which combine the best of both worlds.

(2) **What academic contents and skills should universities teach?**
Graduate attributes should not be envisaged purely in terms of employability, for although this is a prime

focus of university education, it is certainly not the only one. Instead, graduate attributes should include a consideration of what students need to survive in the twenty-first century. We should be preparing students for a world that is increasingly marked by volatility, uncertainty, complexity, and ambiguity. Our graduates should not only have achieved some depth in their area of study but also be able to think effectively and critically, and have an understanding of the ways in which to acquire knowledge of and insight into society and the self. They should be able to use what they gained at university to find creative solutions for pressing local and global issues.

(3) **How will degrees and certification look like in the future?**

Scientific partnerships and cooperation have expanded, not only across regional and disciplinary boundaries but also between academic/research institutions and commerce and industry. This development holds great promise of new avenues for research funding, scholarships, and opportunities for knowledge exchange and internships.

For some years already, we have seen a steady increase in agreements between Stellenbosch University and other universities to offer double and joint degrees – mostly at postgraduate level. This has occurred within the framework of both new and established bilateral partnerships, which hold many mutual benefits to both parties. This kind of collaboration is set to continue, and could be extended to undergraduate (Baccalaureus) level, since we already offer many study-abroad opportunities entailing semester exchanges.

Online learning is likely to increase student mobility virtually, in cyberspace. *The Economist* recently (August 8, 2020 edition) reported that COVID-19 is catalyzing innovation – the Big Ten Academic Alliance, a group of midwestern universities in the United States, is offering many of its 600,000 students the opportunity to take online courses at other universities in the group.

At the same time, different kinds of institutions could start offering courses and end up issuing qualifications. Scott Galloway told *New York Magazine* recently (May 11, 2020), "The post-pandemic future will entail partnerships between the largest tech companies in the world and elite universities (hypothetically, MIT@Google, iStanford, HarvardxFacebook). This will allow universities to expand enrolment dramatically by offering hybrid online-offline degrees, the affordability and value of which will seismically alter the landscape of higher education."

(4) **Who is and what role, according to you, does a university's community play in the future?**
A university's community is very important, but its nature is set to be redefined. At the moment, the university community is made up of all those immediately attached to the institution – i.e., staff and students, but also alumni, donors, the surrounding community (town council, schools, business chambers, tourism structures, religious bodies, NGOs, etc), government (especially structures regulating higher education), the higher education sector (nationally and internationally), research and professional bodies, as well as industry and business. With universities going more and more into cyberspace via online learning, more stakeholders are likely to become part of their community.

(5) **Will the change in higher education be transformative or disruptive, and why? In case of disruption, what could and should universities do to counter their potential disruption?**
Universities may be ripe for disruption but they are also ready for innovation. The challenges they face can be turned into opportunities.

To start with, we have to ensure that we fully optimize our core business – delivering well-qualified graduates, producing relevant research, and having a positive impact on society. Yet that does not mean we can be complacent and carry on with business as usual. Nor does it mean we must throw the baby out with the bathwater.

While online education does not offer a cheaper alternative to face-to-face teaching, as technology costs are an add-on, it does offer scalability. The fact that one is able to serve many more students brings down the unit cost, which makes it more efficient and affordable. And that is the strongest case for universities to expand our e-learning offering (including fully online, blended, and hybrid modes) so that we can dramatically increase our developmental impact where it is needed most.

There is no question that we face immense challenges in higher education. Confronting them will require an equally immense effort. It is best that we take our cue from Daniel Burnham, the American architect who helped rebuild Chicago after the great fire of 1871. He famously said: "Make no little plans; they have no magic to stir [the] blood."

(6) **In summary, how would you describe the university of the twenty-first century?**

The concept of a twenty-first-century university is associated with such features as technology, innovation, the knowledge society, and globalization.

Let's start at the end, globalization: Baumert argues, "While the dominant notion of higher education and universities in particular used to be that of national or sub-national entities (Robertson et al., 2012, p. 7) with clearly defined (local and national) boundaries, we increasingly observe new forms of cross-border institutional interconnectivity that higher education and universities are becoming involved in, which challenge its (sub-)national nature."

There is "talk of borderless or transnational education, education across borders, offshore education and international trade of educational services," which "indicates that processes of internationalization in academia have reached a new quality that goes beyond the traditional physical mobility of people between nation states ... [implying] new modes of higher education provision as well as new forms of inter-institutional collaboration spurred by greater access to knowledge and research, in increasing awareness of international competitiveness and international standing."

Let's turn to technology: The use of learning technologies provides new opportunities to effectively and efficiently extend both the reach and richness of the academic offering. This is achieved through the following:

- Better interaction between lecturers and students, and better feedback on the knowledge levels of individual students.
- Improved access to content resources, so that students can move from consumers to cocreators of their own learning experience.
- Cooperative peer and social learning opportunities through the use of online collaborative tools and the thoughtful use of social media applications in learning and teaching.
- Development of graduate attributes needed for the digital knowledge economy.
- Contribution to the public good by enhancing collaboration among academics.

However, this vision can only be achieved if the following is addressed:

- The academic project and not the technology per se drives the initiatives.

- Technology is not simply used to replicate or serve as an add-on to existing teaching.
- Both lecturers and students are supported to acquire the necessary digital and information literacy and pedagogical skills to facilitate learning in the digital knowledge society.
- A research-based and evaluative approach is used to roll out ICTs in learning and teaching (Baumert, 2014).

REFERENCES

Baumert, S. C. (2014). *University politics under the impact of societal transformation and global processes: South Africa and the case of Stellenbosch University, 1990–2010*. Thesis (PhD). Stellenbosch University, Stellenbosch.

Robertson, S., Dale, R., Moutsios, S., Nielsen, G., Shore, C., & Wright, S. (2012). *Globalisation and regionalisation in higher education: Toward a new conceptual framework*. Aarhus, Denmark: EPOKE, Department of Education, Aarhus University.

ABOUT THE AUTHOR

Andreas Kaplan has more than a decade of leadership experience in the higher education sector. He consecutively served as Rector and Dean of ESCP Business School in Berlin and Paris. Previously, he served as Provost and Dean of Academic Affairs overseeing approximately 6,000 students and supervising nearly 30 degree programs ranging from undergraduate, Master's, and (Executive) MBA, to the School's PhD programs.

Kaplan completed most of his studies and engaged in his professional career alternating between France and Germany. A European at heart, he moreover has resided and worked in Austria, Italy, Portugal, Spain, and the United Kingdom. He is board member of the German-French Economic Circle, part of the prestigious society of leadership fellows of St. George's House – Windsor Castle, as well as a founding member of the European Center for Digital Competitiveness.

Professor Kaplan's research focuses on analyzing the digital world, in particular the areas of artificial intelligence and social media. With several seminal articles and more than 30,000 citations on Google Scholar, Professor Kaplan has been ranked among the top 50 business and management authors worldwide by John Wiley & Sons. Furthermore, a widely covered Stanford study classified Kaplan among the world's most-cited and impactful scientists. Kaplan has teaching experience in top-tier institutions, among them Harvard, Sciences Po Paris, and Tsinghua University.

Regularly serving as keynote speaker and presenter at academic and nonacademic conferences and events, Kaplan's work has been featured in various national and international press and media outlets such as the *California Management Review*, the *Financial Times*, the *Harvard Business Review France*, *La Tribune*, *La Repubblica*, *Süddeutsche Zeitung*, and *die Zeit*. His advisory and consultant activities for a variety of corporations and organizations surround the aforementioned topics.

Professor Kaplan earned his Habilitation at the Sorbonne and his Doctorate at the University of Cologne. He holds an MPA from the École Nationale d'Administration (ENA, Class of République), an MSc from ESCP Business School, and a BSc from Ludwig Maximilian University of Munich. Additionally, Kaplan was visiting PhD at INSEAD and participated in the International Teachers Programme (ITP) at Northwestern University's Kellogg School of Management.

INDEX